THE CREATION MEMOS

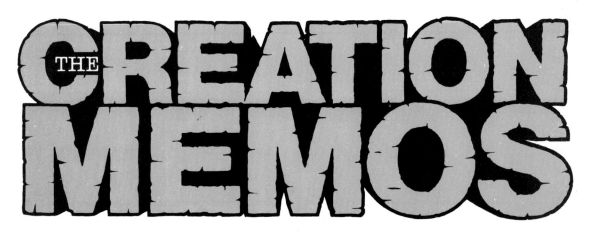

THE CREATION MEMOS

GEOFFREY ATKINSON

PRICE/STERN/SLOAN
Publishers, Inc., Los Angeles

All the characters and companies in this book are imaginary and have no reference to any person, living or dead, or to any real company.

Published by Price/Stern/Sloan Publishers, Inc.
410 North La Cienega Boulevard, Los Angeles, California 90048

ISBN: 0-8431-1031-7

First published in Great Britain 1983

IN THE BEGINNING THERE WAS

...a memorandum

EARLY THIS YEAR ARCHAEOLOGISTS SEARCHING FOR ADDENDA TO THE DEAD SEA SCROLLS UNCOVERED A HUGE OBLONG RECEPTACLE MADE OF A MATERIAL UNLIKE ANYTHING PREVIOUSLY KNOWN. ON IT WAS STENCILED THE HEBREW WORD FOR "CLASSIFIED."

מְהֵימָן,

CARBON DATING PLACE THE RECEPTACLE'S AGE SOMEWHERE BETWEEN EIGHT AND TEN TRILLION YEARS.

AFTER IT WAS CAREFULLY OPENED, THIS REMARKABLE DISCOVERY TURNED OUT TO BE A FILING CABINET FILLED WITH INCREDIBLE DOCUMENTS RELATING TO THE CREATION OF THE WORLD.

ALL CULTURES AND RELIGIONS, OF COURSE, HAVE THEIR OWN LEGENDS EXPLAINING THIS MOMENTOUS EVENT, BUT NOW, AT LAST, THE FACTS ARE AVAILABLE–THE ABSOLUTE TRUTH ABOUT HOW IT ALL STARTED.

From the Desk of "GOD"

Things To Do Today

1. Gift certificate for music lesson for Gabriel.

2. Annual Angel Directors Meeting. 10 A.M.

3. Contact COSMIC FINANCIAL COMMITTEE re: financing new creation WORLD project.

OSMIC FINANCIAL
CORPORATION

BIGGEST IN THE UNIVERSE

TELEPHONE:964359214 to 954359792 (inclusive)
TELEX:AMALWORLDS

enda for Thursday's meeting:

1. Executive stock options and Bonus plan.

2. Lunch.

3. Request from God for financial aid to build New World Project.

COSMIC FINANCIAL
CORPORATION

BIGGEST IN THE UNIVERSE

TELEPHONE:964359214 to 954359792 (inclusive)
TELEX:AMALWORLDS

Dear God:

Our Board has taken up your New World project and okayed same. We do, however, feel strongly that a feasibility study is essential, so as to have no recurrence of the Venus and Mars fiascos. And we insist on dealing directly on this project with you and not with your representative, Lucifer, with whom we had so much past trouble.

Hoping to hear from you soon.

I remain,

Altman Drumm

ALTMAN DRUMM
(Assistant to the President)

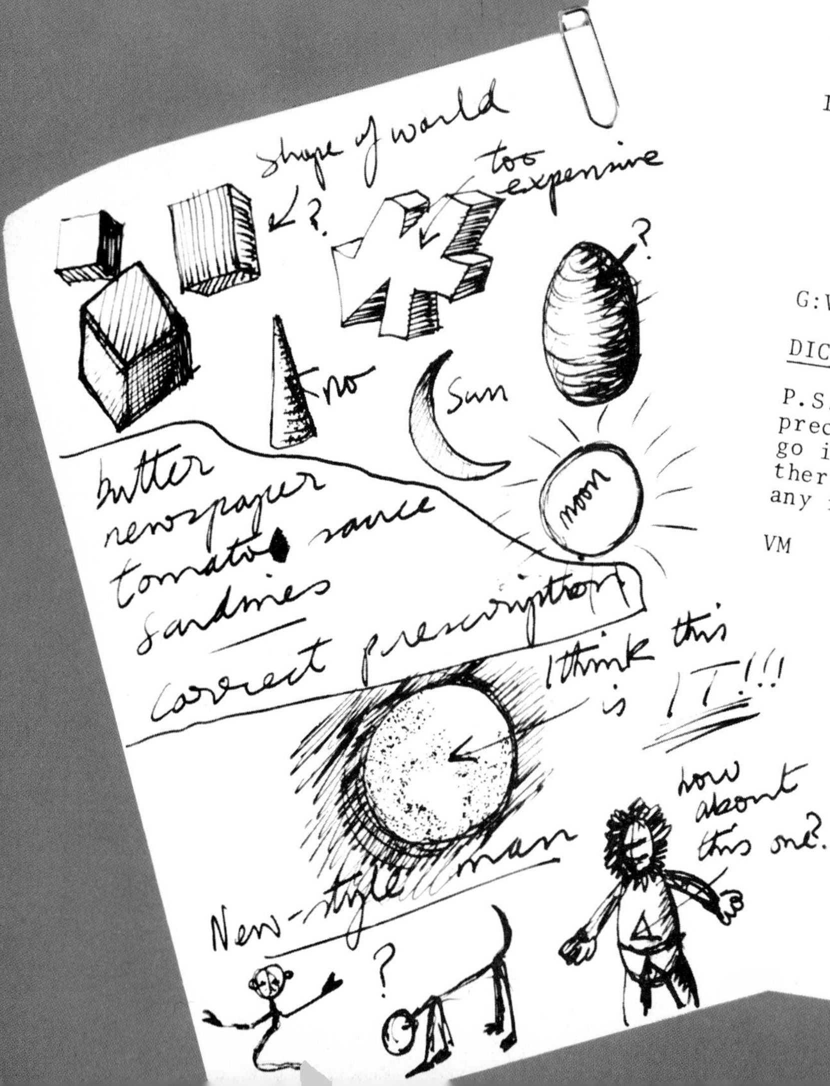

“God”

Dear Mr. Drumm:

Delighted to learn of your inter
We will prepare a feasibility study
enclosed are sketches for prelimina
plans.

Do not worry about Lucifer. He i
longer with our organization.

Yours sincerely,

Veronica Makepiece
for GOD

G:VM

DICTATED BUT NOT READ

P.S. The parting of Lucifer was not
precisely amicable. He is attempting t
go into competition with us. I would
therefore not mention his name to God in
any future correspondence.

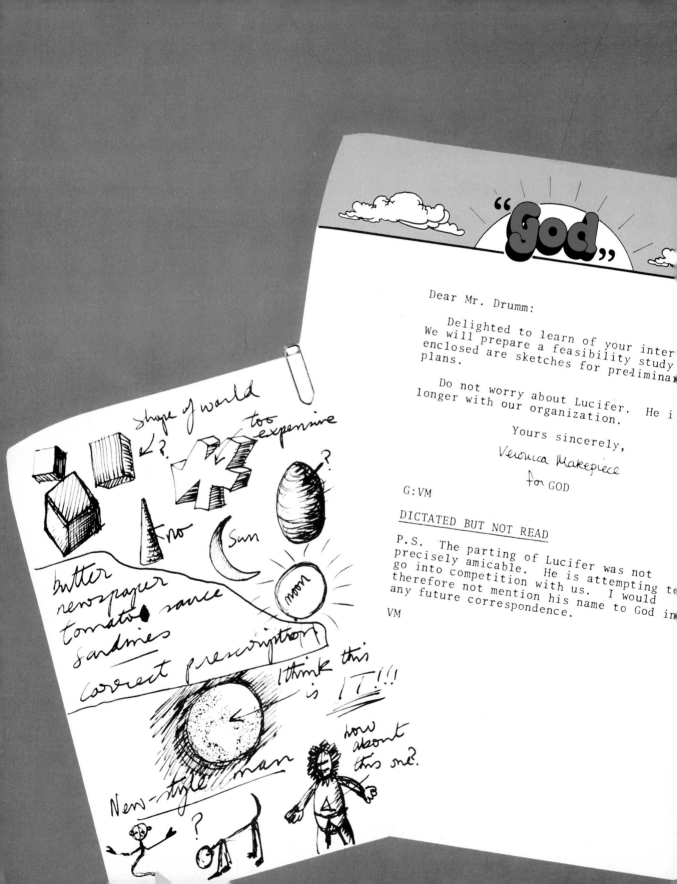

VM

COSMIC FINANCIAL CORPORATION

BIGGEST IN THE UNIVERSE

TELEPHONE:964359214 to 954359792 (inclusive)
TELEX:AMALWORLDS

Dear God:

We are now delighted to be working directly with you through Miss Makepeace. Can you give us a "guesstimate" of the time it may take to complete the world?

I have had a look at your material, some of which seems fine. Meanwhile, here are some of my own thoughts, dashed off at lunch the other day.

Yours truly,

Altman Drumm

ALTMAN DRUMM
(Assistant to the President)

(include sketch)

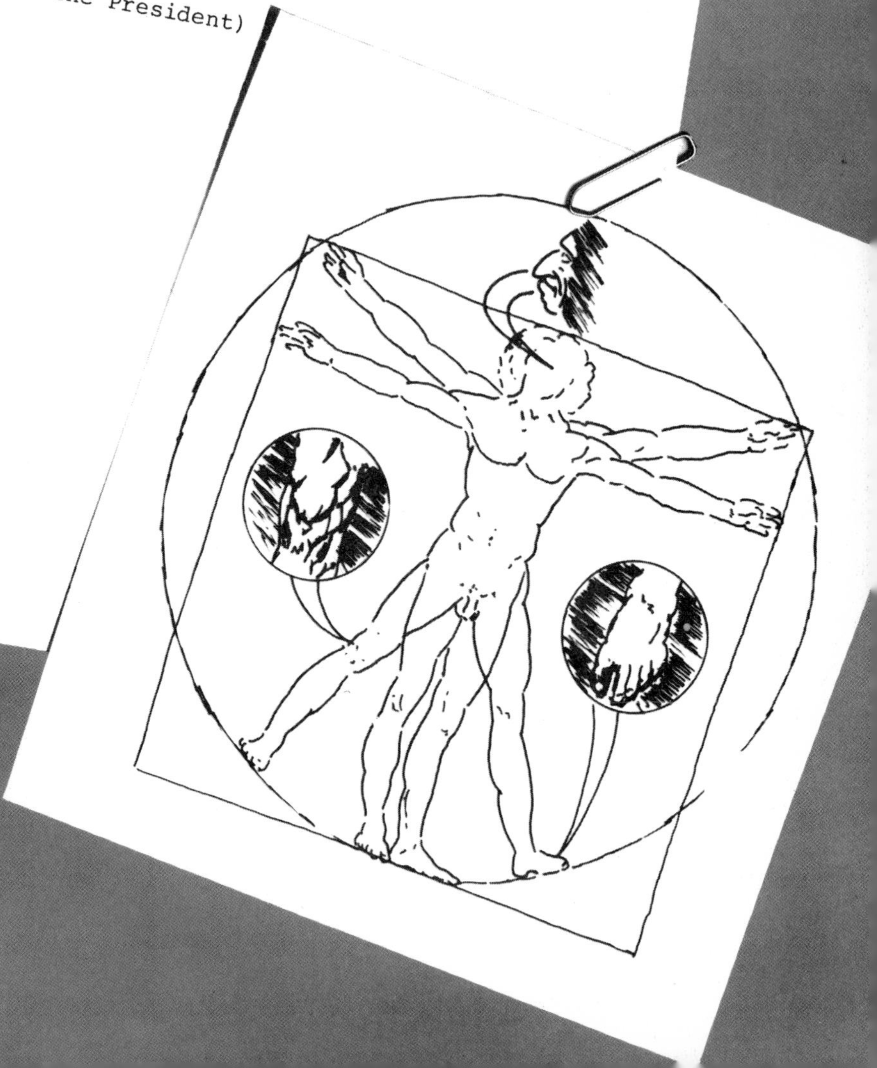

"God"

Dear Mr. Drumm:

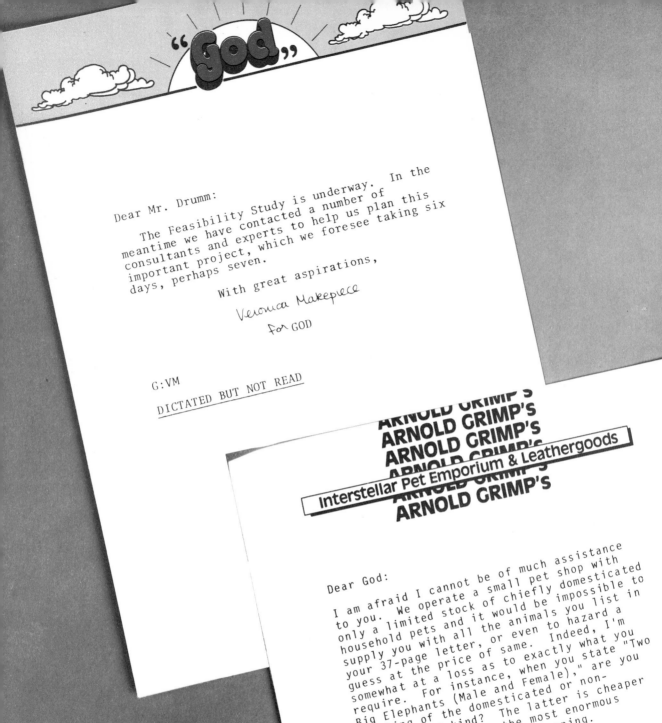

The Feasibility Study is underway. In the meantime we have contacted a number of consultants and experts to help us plan this important project, which we foresee taking six days, perhaps seven.

With great aspirations,

Veronica Makepiece

for GOD

G:VM

DICTATED BUT NOT READ

ARNOLD GRIMP'S
ARNOLD GRIMP'S
ARNOLD GRIMP'S
ARNOLD GRIMP'S
ARNOLD GRIMP'S
ARNOLD GRIMP'S
ARNOLD GRIMP'S

Interstellar Pet Emporium & Leathergoods

Dear God:

I am afraid I cannot be of much assistance to you. We operate a small pet shop with only a limited stock of chiefly domesticated household pets and it would be impossible to supply you with all the animals you list in your 37-page letter, or even to hazard a guess at the price of same. Indeed, I'm somewhat at a loss as to exactly what you require. For instance, when you state "Two Big Elephants (Male and Female)," are you thinking of the domesticated or non-domesticated kind? The latter is cheaper but is apt to cause the most enormous problems, if you take my meaning.

Yours sincerely,

Agnes Grimp

AGNES GRIMP
(Manager)

CONSOLIDATED
WEALTH & PROPERTY
Insurance Advisers and Brokers

Dear God:

I have received your letter concerning the proposed insurance for a new planet you intend to build. May I first thank you for allowing us to quote on this project, and may I also take the opportunity to wish you every success in the venture.

I would like to point out, however, that you ought not to neglect the ever-increasing cost of raw materials. Do not underestimate the cost of such items as rivers and mountains!

Add to this the fact that you intend to populate the earth with a number of "creatures". All these would undoubtedly need personal insurance. And even then there is the question of this "man" you intend to create. Covering him for third party, fire and theft would be quite costly.

Perhaps you could pop into the office next time you're in the neighborhood and we could discuss the project. There are a number of potentially cost-saving ideas you might like to consider. For instance, if the world was registered as a charity you would be able to claim a substantial discount on any premium paid.

Yours sincerely,

Doris Puck

DORIS PUCK
Director
Consolidated Wealth
& Property

Intergalactic
Garden Centre
House Plants and Ecosystems
Our Specialty

Dear God:

Thank you for your letter concerning your proposed new planet. We would of course be delighted to help you stock your "Garden of Eden" and strongly recommend that you contact us before proceeding with any plans.

As to your inquiry about using artificial plants, we feel this would be counter-productive. Your idea about covering the entire surface of your world with concrete certainly simplifies things. But as gardeners we naturally cannot be too enthusiastic. And a giant concrete ball would, you must admit, not be too attractive and would not offer much of a home for the "abundant creatures" you plan to install on your new project.

Your yellow thumb,

WILLIAM B. ASTART
(Sales Manager)

P.S. Have you considered skunk cabbage?

Superfab
Superior Fabrics Ltd.
Consultants in Interior and Exterior Designs

Dear God:

Thank you for writing to us at Superfab with regard to decoration of your forthcoming world.

Right now I am leaning heavily on the idea of a purple, as opposed to a light chartreuse trim. But only for the trees and grass. The sky, of course, will be a divine pink. My dear, pink is absolutely the most fun color we could have!

Naturally, swatches will be sent to you under separate cover and you can make the final choice.

Best,

Ned Tibber

NED TIBBER
Customer Liaison Dept.
SUPERFAB

Valjean, Raskinikov & Attila
CERTIFIED PUBLIC ACCOUNTANTS

Dear God:

Thank you for your letter regarding the new planet you intend to build.

I note that you intend to build the entire world in six days and would point out that, from a financial point of view, you might care to have your income for this work assessed over a three-year period. I would also advise you to consider the timing of this period. By deferring some of the creation until the next fiscal year you would be able to save a considerable amount in taxes.

You might also like to consider setting the whole thing up as a public company and issue shares. This would certainly limit your personal tax liability and might well reduce the overall taxable amount. As a public company you would qualify for numerous extra benefits, and if you were to select an urban redevelopment zone for the site you might well avoid taxes altogether.

In other words this planet which you envisage could turn out to be an excellent tax shelter. However, you must be sure to get waivers from all suppliers, and, as an additional precaution, we suggest that you put the new planet, which you are contemplating naming "Earth," into your mother's name.

Sincerely,

Colin Dull

COLIN DULL
Partner
Valjean, Raskinikov
& Attila

SCHWARTZDIGGER & NEAL

CONSULTATIVE SURVEYORS
Surveys, Valuations,
Estate Management

Dear God:

As to your request, let me say that I'm not altogether familiar with the area to which you refer and a fair price will always depend on the site. However, I feel the figure you quote is not far off the mark, especially if, as you say, it is an up-and-coming area.

For advice on items to be aware of, my best tip would be to have a quiet word with the neighbors. They can usually offer an invaluable source of local knowledge. And do look out for Black Holes. Too many people build worlds on or near Black Holes, only to see them disappear into oblivion within a short time.

Best wishes,

LeRoy Del Schwartzdigger

LEROY DEL SCHWARTZDIGGER
Partner

"God"

Dear Mr. Drumm:

Re: World (The), Creation Of

Please find enclosed legal advice from my attorneys, who have kindly advised me as to the legal aspects of the above project.

As you will see, it does appear to be a particularly cumbersome and involved matter. However, I am confident that, with a little thought, the difficulties mentioned can be successfully overcome.

I trust that the enclosed will be of interest.

Yours sinc

Veronica Mat

GOD

G:VM

DICTATED BUT NOT

SHUSTER, SHYSTER, SUSHI, and POLLOCK

Attorneys at Law

Dear Mr. God:

Creation of World Project

I have studied your letters. And drawings. How talented you are! And what an eye for color! I would never have thought to use orange and green for such a project. How unusual.

I must first advise you that legally you are obliged to adhere to all planning rules and regulations. While you personally - and I quote - "could not give a monkey's ass about zoning", I fear other people with considerable influence could, and will be sure to give you a rough time of it in the not-too-distant future.

Let me therefore outline the legal position for your information:

(1) Planning Permission You should submit plans, stating all relevant dimensions and all construction substances to be used.

(2) Health and Safety You must notify the Health and Safety Commission of the appropriate area as to your intention to build a new world. And you must insure that they are furnished with all necessary information. In particular, they will wish to know whether the world is to have correct sanitation (a particularly important aspect since I see that you intend to install camels.) And they will wish to be made aware of any odors that might be expected to emanate from the world (again, I come back to the camels.) Remember that with a world of this size you will be legally required to provide a minimum number of toilets and wash basins. There is, incidentally, no maximum number.

3) Fire You are legally required, in all worlds intended for multiple occupancy by more than 12 creatures, to provide adequate fire safety precautions, including fire escapes, fire extinguishers, fire buckets, some shiny yellow pants and a rope. In addition, you must prove that the world is constructed with non-combustible substances, in accordance with the latest regulations. I enclose a list of these for your reference.

I would again stress most strongly that legally the owner of a new world must satisfy a number of stringent requirements. Please do not do anything foolish. Just because I am, to use your words, "a well-known and well-liked attorney," it does not mean that I can get you "off the hook, if you catch my drift." The law is the law, and as an attorney I regret that it is my professional duty to abide by it.

Yours lawfully,

R.J. Fiddle

R.J. FIDDLE

FIRE REGULATIONS. USE OF MATERIAL CORRESPONDING TO THE NEW FIRE CODE (1134 through 1187/B)

Sand

Grit

Humus

Protein

Nitrogen

Oxygen (must be contained in metal canister at all times)

Niacin

Acetyl Salicylate

Lecithin

Concrete

Polyester (non-biodegradable)

Chocolate Milkshakes

COSMIC FINANCIAL CORPORATION

BIGGEST IN THE UNIVERSE

TELEPHONE:964359214 to 954359792 (inclusive)
TELEX:AMALWORLDS

Dear God:

Received your note regarding the opinions of your attorney. Do not worry. These details will straighten themselves out once the feasibility report is in place.

In the meantime I thought some of the enclosed business cards, which my secretary found in the back of my desk, might be of interest to you.

Any consideration given to Teddy and Keith Acropolis would be appreciated. They are my wife's cousins.

Very truly yours,

Mark Pederson

MARK PEDERSON
Assistant to Mr. Drumm

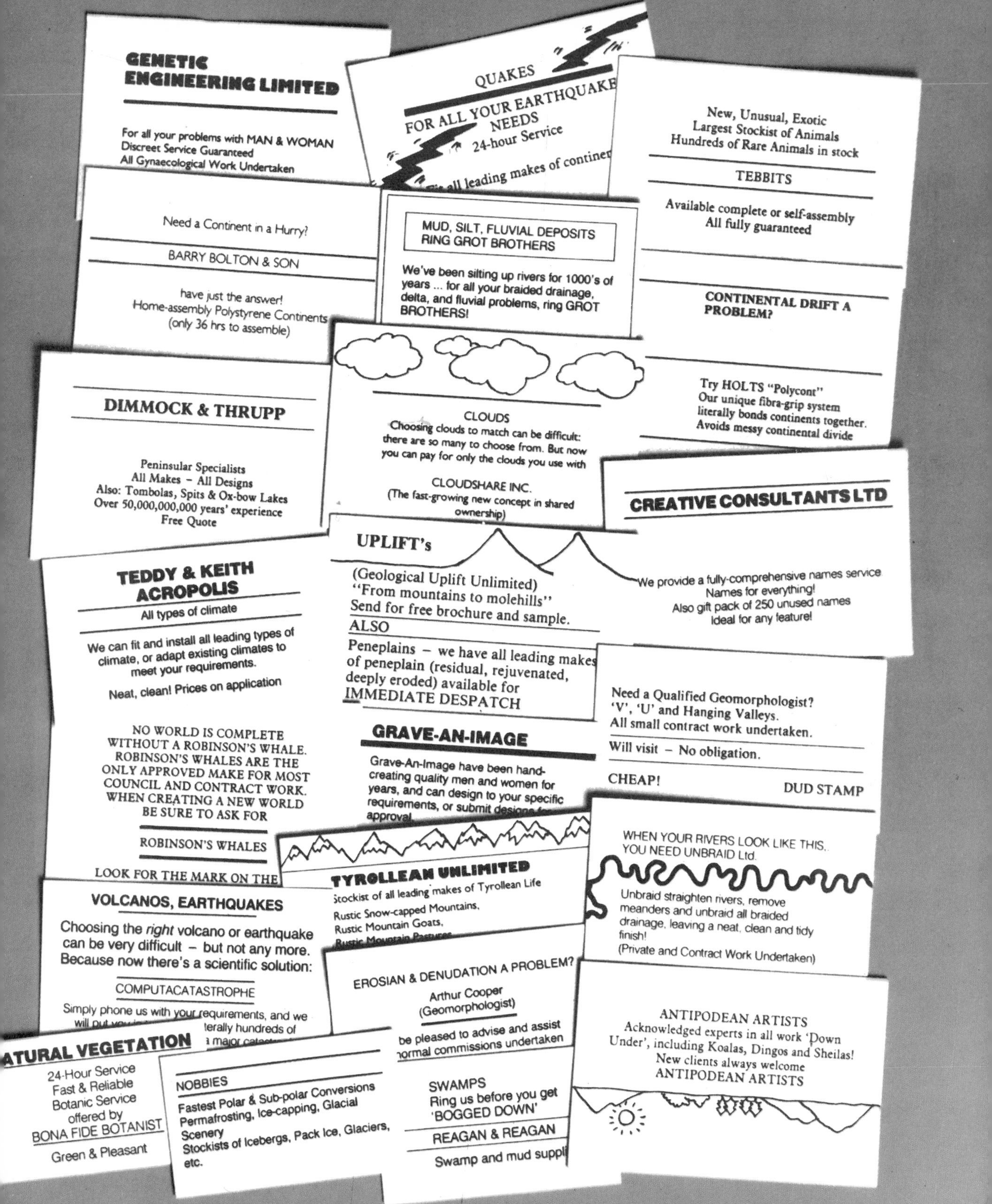
GENETIC ENGINEERING LIMITED
For all your problems with MAN & WOMAN
Discreet Service Guaranteed
All Gynaecological Work Undertaken
QUAKES
FOR ALL YOUR EARTHQUAKE NEEDS
24-hour Service
all leading makes of contine
New, Unusual, Exotic
Largest Stockist of Animals
Hundreds of Rare Animals in stock
TEBBITS
Available complete or self-assembly
All fully guaranteed
Need a Continent in a Hurry?
BARRY BOLTON & SON
have just the answer!
Home-assembly Polystyrene Continents
(only 36 hrs to assemble)
MUD, SILT, FLUVIAL DEPOSITS
RING GROT BROTHERS
We've been silting up rivers for 1000's of years ... for all your braided drainage, delta, and fluvial problems, ring GROT BROTHERS!
CONTINENTAL DRIFT A PROBLEM?
Try HOLTS "Polycont"
Our unique fibra-grip system literally bonds continents together.
Avoids messy continental divide
DIMMOCK & THRUPP
Peninsular Specialists
All Makes – All Designs
Also: Tombolas, Spits & Ox-bow Lakes
Over 50,000,000,000 years' experience
Free Quote
CLOUDS
Choosing clouds to match can be difficult: there are so many to choose from. But now you can pay for only the clouds you use with
CLOUDSHARE INC.
(The fast-growing new concept in shared ownership)
CREATIVE CONSULTANTS LTD
We provide a fully-comprehensive names service
Names for everything!
Also gift pack of 250 unused names
Ideal for any feature!
TEDDY & KEITH ACROPOLIS
All types of climate
We can fit and install all leading types of climate, or adapt existing climates to meet your requirements.
Neat, clean! Prices on application
UPLIFT's
(Geological Uplift Unlimited)
"From mountains to molehills"
Send for free brochure and sample.
ALSO
Peneplains – we have all leading makes of peneplain (residual, rejuvenated, deeply eroded) available for
IMMEDIATE DESPATCH
Need a Qualified Geomorphologist?
'V', 'U' and Hanging Valleys.
All small contract work undertaken.
Will visit – No obligation.
CHEAP!
DUD STAMP
NO WORLD IS COMPLETE WITHOUT A ROBINSON'S WHALE. ROBINSON'S WHALES ARE THE ONLY APPROVED MAKE FOR MOST COUNCIL AND CONTRACT WORK. WHEN CREATING A NEW WORLD BE SURE TO ASK FOR
ROBINSON'S WHALES
LOOK FOR THE MARK ON THE
GRAVE-AN-IMAGE
Grave-An-Image have been hand-creating quality men and women for years, and can design to your specific requirements, or submit designs for approval
WHEN YOUR RIVERS LOOK LIKE THIS, YOU NEED UNBRAID Ltd.
Unbraid straighten rivers, remove meanders and unbraid all braided drainage, leaving a neat, clean and tidy finish!
(Private and Contract Work Undertaken)
TYROLLEAN UNLIMITED
Stockist of all leading makes of Tyrollean Life
Rustic Snow-capped Mountains,
Rustic Mountain Goats,
VOLCANOS, EARTHQUAKES
Choosing the right volcano or earthquake can be very difficult – but not any more. Because now there's a scientific solution:
COMPUTACATASTROPHE
Simply phone us with your requirements, and we
EROSIAN & DENUDATION A PROBLEM?
Arthur Cooper
(Geomorphologist)
be pleased to advise and assist
normal commissions undertaken
ANTIPODEAN ARTISTS
Acknowledged experts in all work 'Down Under', including Koalas, Dingos and Sheilas!
New clients always welcome
ANTIPODEAN ARTISTS
ATURAL VEGETATION
24-Hour Service
Fast & Reliable
Botanic Service
offered by
BONA FIDE BOTANIST
Green & Pleasant
NOBBIES
Fastest Polar & Sub-polar Conversions
Permafrosting, Ice-capping, Glacial Scenery
Stockists of Icebergs, Pack Ice, Glaciers, etc.
SWAMPS
Ring us before you get 'BOGGED DOWN'
REAGAN & REAGAN
Swamp and mud suppli

"God"

Re: Creation of A World

I am sorry that the feasibility study has not yet been forthcoming. I have been away from the office for some time with a severe attack of nasal colic. Rest assured I will now devote my energies to the task of obtaining the necessary study.

With kind regards,

Veronica Makepiece
For
God

COSMIC FINANCIAL CORPORATION

BIGGEST IN THE UNIVERSE

TELEPHONE 964359214 to 954359792 inclusive
TELEX AMALWORLDS

My Dear God:

Re: Creation of a World

You may recall that some ten weeks ago we agreed that you would arrange with an appropriate company to furnish me with a feasibility study into the prospect of creating a new world.

I see from our records that this study is yet to be forthcoming and I wonder if you could look into the matter for me.

Trusting you will report back at your earliest convenience.

Yours as ever,

Altman Drumm

ALTMAN DRUMM

FROGGINS, FROGGINS, & FROGGINS.
Consultants and Business Research

Dear God.

We received your drawing of "Man". We like the general idea but do not understand the small lever in the center. Is this for tilting him forward or backward? Or some kind of fuel intake? Please advise.

High-quality
PRUDEHOMME
Research

Dear God:

We regret to inform you that we must refuse to continue with research on your World project. After seeing your idea for the creature you call "Man," we were all shocked and disgusted by the picturization of the uncovered lobes. You cannot expect us to ask any of the decent ladies in our shop to work on such obscene garbage.

If you eliminate these exposed lobes, we might consider continuing.

Respectfully,

Brian Prudehomme

BRIAN PRUDEHOMME

N'S CON'S CON'S CON'S CON

(Incorporating Consolidated Money,
Consolidated Wealth, Consolidated Bank Accounts,
Consolidated Bags of Loose Change)

Dear God:

RE: Creation Of A World

Thank you for your request that we undertake a small feasibility study for you. Regretfully, we cannot oblige. We are moving offices, our present accommodation having been mysteriously engulfed in a dreadful fire not a week ago.

It is ironical that, on the previous occasions you have been in touch with me, I have had to turn down your requests for similar reasons. It does appear that my ill-luck with fires and floods is matched only by my foresight in negotiating insurance coverage.

Apologies again for not being able to offer you assistance. Perhaps I will have more time when my wife and I return from our forthcoming 60-day cruise.

With all best wishes,

Aarfon Growbag

AARFON GROWBAG

NOMENCLATURE RESEARCH

Dear God,

Re: Creation of A World

Thank you for your letter. What a pleasure it was to hear from you after such a long time. And how very interesting - a new world. You must be very excited. I fear though that we will not be in a position to help you with your intended feasibility study. We have just recently closed our 'property consultancy' office after a somewhat troublesome inquiry by the local police: an inquiry about which I feel most bitter.

We are now, as it happens, in the process of opening a 'pre-owned vehicle allocation agency', which I feel sure will prove to be a great success. Perhaps you would like to drop by when next in this area. We do from time to time find vehicles which have become unavoidably separated from their owners and need a hasty reallocation, and I feel sure we could find something to suit you.

Trusting you are fit and well.

Yours dodgily,

Flash Stan & Fingers Picklock

Grump, Gromp, McCulloch
Research Partners

Dear God:

Your request for assistance has been received with shock and dismay. Perhaps it has escaped your attention that settlement is required on no less than <u>eight</u> outstanding accounts, and that legal action is pending on four of these.

I suggest that all sums be paid post-haste, if not sooner. I'd like to take this opportunity to remind you that we are a registered business, not a registered charity, and like all other businesses depend upon prompt and early settlement of accounts to remain solvent. You, for your part, seem to operate under some totally different rules.

Until there is some noticeable change, we shall have no cause whatsoever to discuss "exciting new projects". Other than in the Courts.

Yours sternly,

Lionel Gromp

LIONEL GROMP

Dear Mr. Cohen:

RE: Creation of World

Please find enclosed the feasibility study for the World. I very much regret it is not quite as I had envisaged it, but unfortunately every firm I contacted about the work seemed unable to render assistance. I was, alas, therefore compelled to use a company I have never dealt with before. (Nor, I might add, will ever deal with again!)

Please accept my most sincere apologies for what has turned out to be something well below the very high standards which I know you uphold.

Yours,

Veronica Makepiece

for GOD

G:VM

DICTATED BUT NOT READ

CRUDE & OFFENSI

(Established 20 minutes ag

Dear Mister God:

Please find enclosed the study what you asked us to prepare. We're sorry it' dkdkdjkjfj a bit scruffy . But the cat got hold of it, and since we knew you were in such a hurry, we didn't want to waste time re-doing it.

Full settlement within 2½ days.

Yours truly,

R. S. J. Girder

R.S. J. GIRDER

We have been asked by our clients to advise on the creation of a new world, and would report accordingly:

1. We're not sure what <u>shape</u> would be best. But we think roundish would be okay. Though maybe a few corners. Or maybe not. But we think it should definitely be the shape you think it should be.
2. <u>Color</u> We xdxdXdX would suggest a good color be used. Probably one that you think is good.
3. We would suggest you choose an appropriate <u>size</u> for the world. A sort of average size. Although it could maybe be a shade larger . Maybe you could have a few words with someone else and see what they think. That's what we always do.
4. <u>Surface</u> The world should definitely have one.
5. <u>Trees</u> The world should definitely have a few trees knocking around to make it look pretty.
6 <u>Acne</u> The world should not have acne.
7. <u>Trees with acne</u> The world should not have trees with acne.
8 <u>Smell</u> The world shouldn't be too smelly, otherwise no one will want to live there. Except people who like living in smelly places. And let's face it, who wants that sort of person living in their world.

That concludes our feasibility study. If there are any further questions we wouldn't mind answering them. As long as they're not too difficult. And as long as they don't involve us having to write a reply.

COSMIC CORPORATION

BIGGEST IN THE UNIVERSE

TELEPHONE:964359214 to 954359792 (inclusive)
TELEX:AMALWORLDS

Dear God:

I have recently returned to my office after several days off and upon my return was presented with your most recent letter and enclosures.

I do indeed agree that the feasibility study was inadequate in all respects. I have incidentally taken the precaution of destroying the report before anyone here should read it and perhaps gain the impression that we were entertaining incompetency.

Meanwhile, might I suggest the work be put out to bid. At least this way we might obtain some indication of the possible cost. I have therefore requested a specification and draft form be prepared and enclose herewith for your reference.

With kind regard

T.G. Cohe

T.G. COHEN
Project Develo
Officer

B I D S

Bids are hereby invited
for the Creation of
ONE WORLD

Cosmic Financial Corporation are considering the possibilities of creating a brand new world-like structure and invite interested parties to submit full bids for all aspects of the work on or before the last day of this month. All applicants should be fully conversant with world construction and have demonstrable skills to the same.

Work to consist of ONE WORLD of rock, sand and water construction, having circular shape and estimated weight of 6,000,000,000,000,000,000,000 tons and volume of 250,000,000,000 cubic miles. Or thereabouts. DIMENSIONS AND AREA of the world should have girth not exceeding 25,000 miles and revolve about itself on a sealed, maintenance-free bearing. WORLD to incorporate regular orbital system with other planets and not requiring other such planets to be moved. Applicants should supply a separate design specification for separating waters and a plan using waters in a 2:1 relation with land to create a pleasing and acceptable series of continents. Design should include fullest range of currently accepted geographical features. Applicants will be further expected to include their intention for heating and lighting the world.

Sundry items Bids should include full price and details for sundry items as detailed on the specification sheet and wherever so should specify all work to be contracted out with the name of said contractor. Sundry items will include: DESERTS.

PENINSULAS, MOUNTAINS, VOLCANOS, ANTS, CAVES, GLACIAL FEATURES, RIVERS, LAKES, WATERFALLS, BADGERS ... and to include adequate provision for future development and/or modification to customer's requirements. Bids should include price for a full range of fish and aquatic animals.

Man Bids to include a separate price for the provision of a man and a woman to live on the world.

Lighting and heating Lighting is to be on an integral sun and moon system and should again provide for maintenance-free running. A convector system is preferred for all air circulation.

Terms and conditions Preference will be given to bids specifying the shortest possible period of construction. Applicants should also be prepared to issue 12-month guarantees on all parts and labor.

Further particulars and formal bids should be submitted to:

GOD
Agent General
COSMIC FINANCIAL CORP

COSMIC SPECIFICATION SHEET

Dividing light from darkness

Firmament (one)

Dividing waters (under firmament)

Gathering together waters

Gathering together dry land in one place

Bringing forth grass, herb yielding seed and fruit, tree yielding fruit after its kind whose seed is in itself, upon the earth

Installing light

Installing gas and electricity

Dividing days, years, seasons (to customer's specifications)

Making stars (approximately two gross)

Bringing forth fowl that may fly above the earth

Creating whales, living creatures, winged fowl

Creating quiet little coves with sandy beaches

Creating funny little bits of land that stick out into the sea

Creating other bits of land that look as though they're going to fall down at any minute

Creating nice places for picnics

Bringing forth cattle, creeping things, beasts of the earth, and hamsters

Creating man

From rib of man create one woman (subject to availability)

"God"

Dear Mr. Cohen:

You wouldn't believe the prices some of these suppliers are asking.

I have enclosed some of the estimates. Great Me Almighty. Look at those prices.

You are more versed in business than I am. Don't you know any discount suppliers, at least for the flora? Or have you any wholesale contacts?

Let me know.

Yours in haste,

Veronica Makepiece

for GOD

G:VM

DICTATED BUT NOT READ

MURPHY AND MURPHY LTD
Formerly Murphy and Murphy

Dear Sirs:

Re: Your Advertisement

Please see our price below. We trust that it meets your requirements.

		Universal $
97,000,000,000,000,000,000,000,000,000 tons of peat		37
Delivery of above	9,724,134,600	
TOTAL:	9,724,134,637	

WORLDS UNLIMITED

Please find enclosed our estimate for your recently advertised project.

		Universal Dollars
Dry wall mud	94,000	"
Spackling	84,000	"
Plastic wood	71,000	"
Creosote	11,000	"
Rubber bands	87,000	"
Glue	50,000	"
Wall trim	111,000	"
6 in. nails	32,000	"
Elastic bands	1	"
Gravel	0.90	"
Labor	0.21	"
Sub total	538,002.11	"
Sales tax @ 15%	80,700.32	"
	618,702.43	Universal Dollars

Fforbes Browne
HIGH CLASS ARTEFACTS FOR THE GENTRY

Herewith our considered estimate for the work required

46,000,000,000,000,000 million square miles Axminster carpets	99 million guineas
25,000 solid gold trees and assorted vegetation	38 million guineas
94 million rolls Limestone scenery	47 million guineas
6 variable-flow waterfalls	3 million guineas
Fur coat and jewelery (for woman)	·1 million guineas
TOTAL	190 million guineas
tip	10 million guineas
	200 million guineas

EXOTIC WORLDS

ESTIMATE

We have pleasure in supplying our price for your recently advertised project and would advise you of our price as follows:

	Universal Dollars
94,000 tons mixed nuts	
1,400,000 tons brown sugar	71,000
9,000,000,000,000,000 gallons sour cream	9,000
82,000 tons dried carrots (organically grown)	111,000
1,800,000 tons garlic	
1 egg	30,000
Labor	11,000
Sales Tax	319,000
Service	44,900
Sub (sub) total	449,000
Cover charge	130,000
Subtotal	44,900
TOTAL	47,390
	1,269,190

The Amazing Marco

Conjuring Artiste Extraordinaire

ONE WORLD

In accordance with the instructions issued by your company, I am attaching the terms of 1 (one) evening performance in which to conjure up the required article.

Labor	94 dollars
Assistant's labor	6 dollars
Insurance	250,000 dollars
TOTAL:	250,100 dollars

(Rabbits, doves, etc., extra)

goldberg's
"To you, my son"

OUR QUOTATION

Enclosed for you our estimate for preparing a high quality, de luxe world. If we can be of help, ring us and without delay we will be round.

1 kosher firmament	45,000,000	shekels
1 kosher selection of beasts that creepeth	2,000,000	"
1 kosher whale	48	"
selection of finest kosher grass and herb yielding seed	3,100	"
97,000,000 synagogues	96,000,000	"
1 man (of the faith)	2,000,000,000,000	"
1 woman (of the faith)	2,000,000,000,000	"
TOTAL:	4,000,143,003,148	shekels

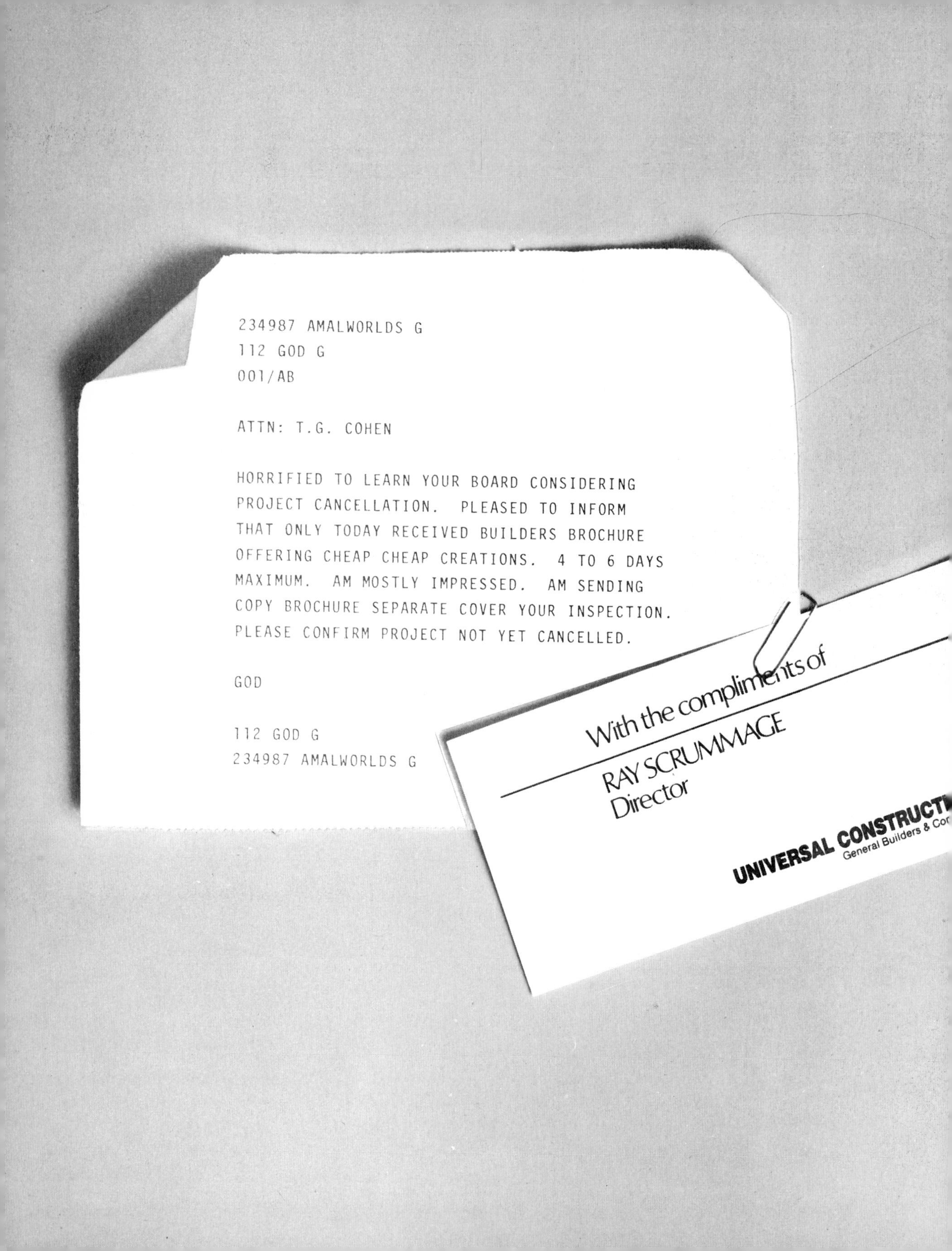
234987 AMALWORLDS G
112 GOD G
001/AB

ATTN: T.G. COHEN

HORRIFIED TO LEARN YOUR BOARD CONSIDERING PROJECT CANCELLATION. PLEASED TO INFORM THAT ONLY TODAY RECEIVED BUILDERS BROCHURE OFFERING CHEAP CHEAP CREATIONS. 4 TO 6 DAYS MAXIMUM. AM MOSTLY IMPRESSED. AM SENDING COPY BROCHURE SEPARATE COVER YOUR INSPECTION. PLEASE CONFIRM PROJECT NOT YET CANCELLED.

GOD

112 GOD G
234987 AMALWORLDS G

With the compliments of
RAY SCRUMMAGE
Director
UNIVERSAL CONSTRUCT
General Builders & Co

UNIVERSAL CONSTRUCTION CO

Loft conversion • Stone cladding • Re-roofing • Damp coursing • Volcanic activity • Plumbing • Continental drifting • Pre-Cambrian uplift • Wet rot treatment • Rewiring • Glaciation • Swimming pools • Double glazing • Igneous intrusions • Repointing • Dividing firmaments • Dividing light from darkness • Crazy paving

BEFORE **AFTER**

- **BEASTS THAT CREEPETH...** Universal Construction Co. install all makes of beasts that creepeth *at competitive rates*
- **DIVIDING FIRMAMENTS...**Firmaments divided or modified
- **QUALIFIED FITTERS...**All our fitters are qualified
- **NO MESS...**We clean up afterwards
- **CHOICE OF FINISHES**

...UNIQUE SIX-DAY CREATION PACKAGE...

All our work is fully guaranteed for 6 months. If in that time you are dissatisfied, just return the world to us and we will refund your money.

CHOICE OF ANTI-CLOCKWISE AND CLOCKWISE ROTATION!

MAINTENANCE FREE

Unsolicited testimonials:

"I purchased one of your worlds two years ago and would recommend them to anyone" — *Mr. R.J. Leviticus*

"In twenty years I have purchased over 500 worlds and can honestly say I have never found one to rival yours" — *Mr. Genuine*

"Hours of fun and amusement" — *Mrs. B.C.*

"Rotten!" — *Mr. & Mrs. Z.*

CHOICE OF COLOURS (No extra charge)
Purple, skin, tan, natural, green, blue, ochre, brilliant white, metallic black, bronze, cream

SIX-DAY PACKAGE

Our unique six-day creation package is a special service to first-time creators. Starting on Monday, we guarantee to complete all work by the following Saturday... or before! Simple. Quick. Effective. No frills. No gimmicks. How do we do it? Simple – we use an efficient team of skilled workers. And only the latest tools and materials.

FREE MOUNTAINS
One free mountain chain with every continent you buy through us

UNIQUE FOUR-DAY MINI-CREATION PACKAGE

Our four-day plan includes division of light and darkness and parting of the waters. But no animals, no herbs and no seeds. And no man. The mini-creation plan is ideal where money is tight or time restricted. Ideal for long weekend! Same quality of workmanship assured.

UNIQUE TEN-DAY DE LUXE CREATION PACKAGE

If you've got more time and want a slightly more sophisticated world, then the ten-day package is ideal. All work as for six-day plan, plus extra man, towns and motorways.

OR

3 CREATIONS FOR THE PRICE OF 2

All the worlds we create are available in kit form for self-assembly and come complete with full instructions.

Like to hear more? Then fill in this coupon:

Name ....

Company ....

Position ....

Address ....

I am interested in: *(tick as applicable)*

☐ Loft Conversions ☐ Dividing Firma...

☐ Re-roofing ☐ Creatio...

UNIVERSAL CONSTR...
Directors: Ray Scrummage, Ted S...

...EST PRICES!

```
112 GOD G
234987 AMALWORLDS G
0001/AB

ATTN: GOD

CONFIRM PROJECT STILL ALIVE
AWAIT DEVELOPMENTS.


T.G. COHEN
234987 AMALWORLDS G
112 GOD G
```

UNIVERSAL CONSTRUCTION CO.
General Builders & Contractors

3rd Arch Along
Limepit Viaduct
Telephone 18194804612 (one line)
Telex CONU

MEMBER OF THE FEDERATION OF SMALL BUILDERS
AND BUILDING CONTRACTORS

Dear God:

Re: Creation of World.

Thank you for your inquiry. Of course we would be delighted to quote for building you a world. Perhaps, though, I should point out at this juncture that we ourselves haven't actually as yet built a complete world, though we have seen lots of pictures and read lots of books about it. However, I feel sure that, given our considerable experience in remodeling, together with a touch of luck, we shall have no problem.

Of course you ought to realize that all building work is much the same. And that just because a firm hasn't perhaps the experience of a more established outfit, it isn't any drawback.

Building is just like riding a bike. Or sex. I mean, you never know till you've tried. But once you've tried you never forget. And you never fall off again either.

In any case we can help with your creation.

What's more, we'll give you a free quote first. And we don't overcharge.

Yours enthusiastically,

Ray Scrummage

RAY SCRUMMAGE
Universal Construction Co.

“God”

Dear Mr. Cohen:

Re: Creation of the World

I have just received a reply from Universal Construction Company. I have looked through the dictionary twice now and still can't quite find a word to describe my reaction.

It would appear that they've never actually built a world, and that the nearest they have come to it is, in fact, a set of ornamental fountains with a dolphin in the middle. Apparently they've never written a letter either. At least not one with decent grammar.

However - and that is a big however - they are enthusiastic. And they're cheap.

Do we pursue the matter?

Yours concernedly,

Veronica Makepiece

G:VM for GOD

DICTATED BUT NOT READ

TELEPHONE:964359214 to 954359792 (inclusive)
TELEX:AMALWORLDS

Dear God:

Re: Creation of World

I've just read your letter and, while one applauds enthusiasm, one needs to temper it with a little realism.

I'm sure Universal Construction mean well - but creating a completely new world is a tricky business.

I have decided to ask you to request that the builders supply us with their fullest estimate and schedule. Only this way can we realistically assess whether the involvement of this firm is viable. We cannot afford mistakes.

Yours cautiously,

T. G. Cohen

T.G. COHEN
Project Development Officer

COSMIC FINANCIAL CORPORATION

BIGGEST IN THE UNIVERSE

TELEPHONE:964359214 to 954359792 (inclusive)
TELEX:AMALWORLDS

Dear God:

Re: Creation of World

On second thought, I don't know that it would be quite such a good idea for Universal Construction to do the work. Enthusiasm and zeal are all very well, but together they are no substitute for experience. I hate to pour cold water on the whole thing but, after a sleepless night considering the project, I fear it would not be at all prudent for Universal Construction to waste their/your/my everyone's time.

I therefore beg you do ask them not to involve themselves any further. Perhaps you could think up a suitable excuse. I know you are very good at this sort of thing.

Yours regretfully,

T. G. Cohen

T.G. COHEN
Project Development Officer

COSMIC FINANCI
CORPORATION

BIGGEST IN THE UNIVERSE

TELEPHONE:964359214 to 954359792 (inclusive)
TELEX:AMALWORLDS

Dear God:

Re: Creation of World

I was suddenly struck by the absurd
my last letter. Of course the proj
important. Of course we can't affo
lose. Of course Universal Construc
must be made aware of the importanc
the work at hand. But we are at th
only talking of estimates and possi

Might I ask you speak to your man a
company, asking him to quote. Make
there are no promises. And that yo
nothing in writing.

Yours sincerely,

T. G. Cohen

T.G. COHEN
Project Development Officer

"God"

Dear Mr. Cohen:

Re: Creation Of The World

I have at long last discovered a company that offers good, reasonably-priced insurance deals. And while I'm sure cost is not everything with a project of this importance, it is at least comforting to know we may be able to make a small saving on our budget.

With best wishes,

Veronica Makepeace

For GOD

G:VM

DICTATED BUT NOT READ

ge
es.

IVOR GOLDFILLING & V.V. RICHE
INSURANCE BROKERS

INSURING A WORLD?
Nowadays, more and more people are buying and furnishing new worlds. Yet how many take the trouble to arrange adequate insurance? In our experience very, very few. All too often a brand new world can be lost **FOREVER** in an accident – and it can never be replaced, *only* because the correct insurance cover hasn't been arranged. This is where we come in! We've been arranging insurance for worlds for a long time, which is why we're able to offer you such a **COMPETITIVE SERVICE.** And at such **COMPETITIVE PRICES!**

Just look what we can offer you:

- **FULLY COMPREHENSIVE INSURANCE ON WORLD** and contents.
- **SPARE WORLD** In the event of your own world being damaged or destroyed, we offer you **AT NO EXTRA CHARGE** a comparable world of comparable size and status for use while yours is out of commission.
- **LOW PREMIUMS** for some professions. Certain low-risk professions such as lawyers, doctors, 'French models' and chiropodists qualify for a **SPECIAL** low premium.
- **LIFE INSURANCE** for all pets, animals, and beasts that do bear the seed. Subject only to an initial medical and/or veterinary report.

Individual needs differ and we try to match each creator's needs with **THE BEST POLICY AVAILABLE.** Perhaps you'd like to drop into our office for a chat so that we can discuss matters further.

Ivor Goldfilling

BODDLERS ASSURANCE COMPANY LIMITED

The Company agrees with the policyholder to provide insurance as expressed in this policy during any period in respect of which the policyholder has paid the premium (see very boring notes at rear of document.)

Definition of The World

For the purposes of the insurance the expression "World" used herein shall mean a large round blob described in 1(a) Description of Blobs in the "Certificate of World Insurances" (hereinafter referred to in this Policy as "The Certificate".) (The rest of this paragraph has been deleted due to lack of space.) (And interest.)

THE POLICYHOLDER'S ATTENTION IS PARTICULARLY DRAWN TO CONDITION 9/64/567/A(b)/23/az (357862) OF THIS POLICY

Insurance Provided

1. Where the Insurance Provided is comprehensive, all clauses of this policy are applicable.

2. Where the Insurance Provided is 'third party, fire and theft' only, Clauses III, IV, V and VII of this policy are not applicable, and Clauses I and XXXII apply only in respect of loss or damage to the world caused directly by fire, self-ignition, lightning, explosion, theft, or attempted theft. In addition, Clause XX applies only in respect of damage caused by theft, fire, flood, locusts, combustible stolen locusts, enormous plagues of haddocks and exploding rice pudding. Clause XVI doesn't apply unless you're a haddock. Clause IX applies on Mondays and alternate Tuesdays.

Loss of or damage to The World

Clause 1

The Company will pay for the loss of or damage to the World (including its accessories and spare parts or components. But not including spare accessories or spare components. Except spare components with no spare accessories.) Payment may be made at the Company's option either for the full cost of repair, reinstatement or replacement, or by cash for the amount of the loss or damage agreed between the Company and the Policyholder, but not in any event exceeding the reasonable market value at the time of the loss or damage (the rest of this paragraph has been deleted due to lack of sense).

wing Charges

ne Company will also pay the reasonable cost f protection and removal to the nearest epairers, if as a result of any loss or damage insured under this Clause the world is disabled.

The Company will not pay for:

a. Depreciation, wear and tear, mechanical or electrical breakdown, or anything else whatsoever.

b. Anything else at all not covered in (a.) above.

c. Damage by overeating.

d. Damage by vandals.

Clause II

There is no Clause II.

The Insured Person

Clause VII

For the purposes of insurance under this condition the term "Insured Person" (as distinct from "Insured Haddock") shall mean any one or more of the following:

a. The Policyholder.

b. Any person using the World with the permission of the Policyholder for social, domestic and pleasure purposes, where such use is permitted by the terms of this Certificate.

c. Not applicable.

Clause IX

The Company will pay for any loss of, or damage to, rugs, clothing and personal effects occurring in or on the World by fire, theft, or sexual activity.

GENERAL EXCEPTIONS

Any liability which attaches by virtue of an agreement but which would not have attached in the absence of such agreement (for further details see lawyer attached to rear of this document).

"God"

Dear Mr. Cohen

Re: Creation of World

I am enclosing herewith the first proposals from Universal Construction. I'm not sure they are quite what we envisaged. In fact, I'm fairly sure they're not. I should also point out that the lurid lime green Pentel of the original copy has not reproduced particularly well.

Trusting that you are now fully recovered from your attack of shingles.

Yours faithfully,

Tanya Starr

PP. God

Enclosures

UNIVERSAL CONSTRUCTION CO.

General Builders & Contractors

3rd Arch Along
Limepit Viaduct
Telephone 18194804612 (one line)
Telex CONU

MEMBER OF THE FEDERATION OF SMALL BUILDERS AND BUILDING CONTRACTORS

Dear Mr. God,

Thank you for your letter. We quite understand the obligation which you stress in your 11-page letter and 3-page synopsis (with 1½ pages of footnotes). And we fully appreciate the importance of this project which is described so comprehensively in the 36-page letter from your solicitor.

With due regard to all that was said therein, we now supply herewith our rough designs and estimates. Plus our suggested 'Six-Day Plan'.

We trust that these will meet with your approval.

Yours faithfully,

Gwyn MacTaggart (Secretary)

Gwyn MacTaggart
Dictated by Mr. Scrummage
and signed in his absence

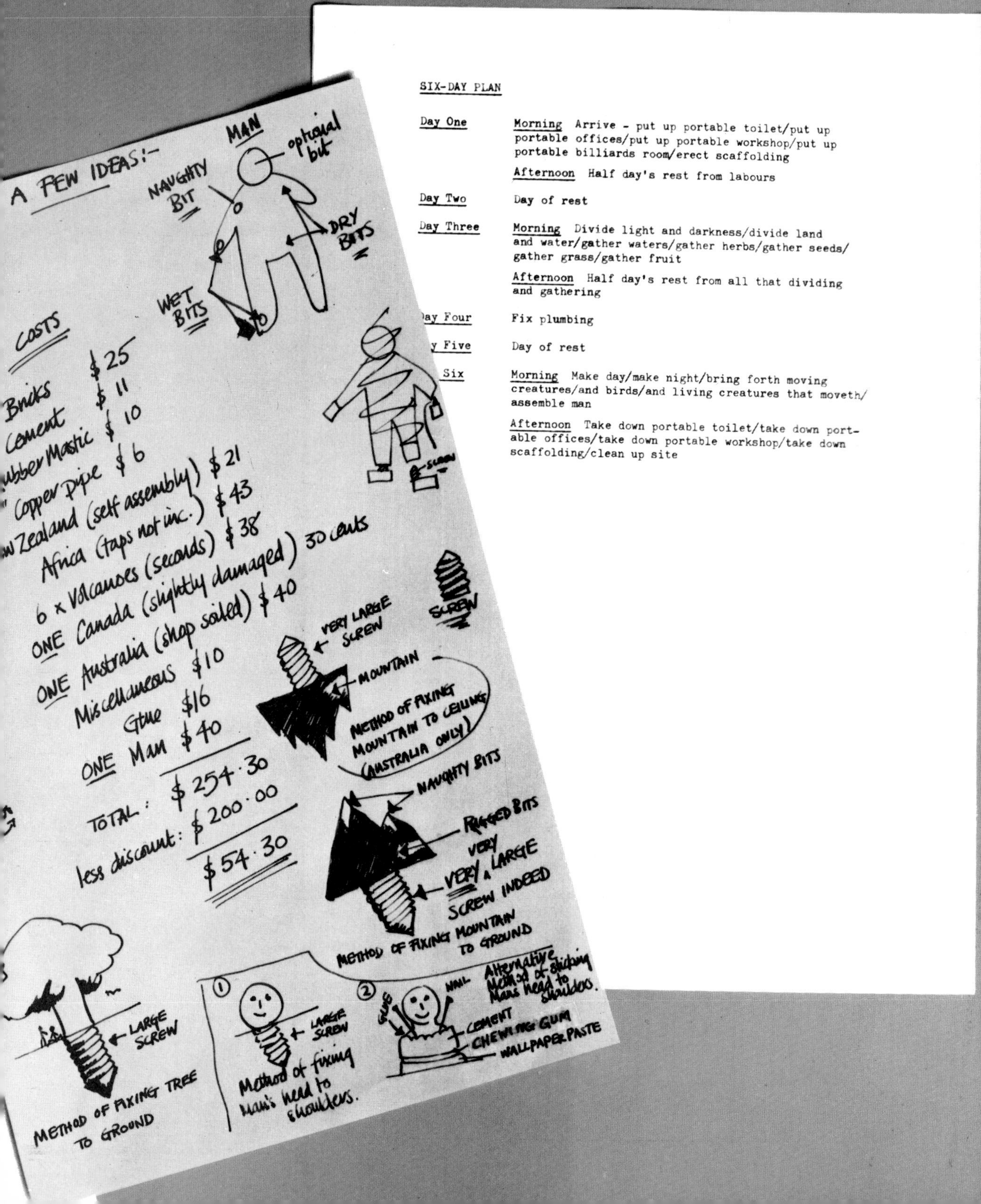

SIX-DAY PLAN

Day One	Morning	Arrive - put up portable toilet/put up portable offices/put up portable workshop/put up portable billiards room/erect scaffolding
	Afternoon	Half day's rest from labours
Day Two		Day of rest
Day Three	Morning	Divide light and darkness/divide land and water/gather waters/gather herbs/gather seeds/gather grass/gather fruit
	Afternoon	Half day's rest from all that dividing and gathering
ay Four		Fix plumbing
y Five		Day of rest
Six	Morning	Make day/make night/bring forth moving creatures/and birds/and living creatures that moveth/assemble man
	Afternoon	Take down portable toilet/take down portable offices/take down portable workshop/take down scaffolding/clean up site

“God”

Dear Mr. Cohen:

Re: Creation of The World

Last time I wrote to you, you will recall I was a little worried by the direction in which the proposals from the Universal Construction Company appeared to be moving.

I am afraid these proposals have now become cause for further alarm. I wrote to Mr. Scrummage, the man handling the work for Universal Construction, pointing out that the extensive use of wood and nails, while structurally sound, was not likely to appeal to the aesthetic eye, and requesting they incorporate more flair into their designs.

It was with some surprise, therefore, that I received a somewhat curt reply pointing out that flair costs money and that they personally couldn't see anything wrong with the designs.

I suggested they might supply us with another batch of proposals, which duly arrived on my desk this morning. I regret that they only served to confirm my worst fears. I have drafted a long letter to Mr. Scrummage to try and clear matters up. Here, for your reference, are the proposals as laid out by Universal Construction Company.

On a more favorable note, I have discovered a company that constructs ready-made men. The results seem promising and I have arranged a meeting with a representative from the company to discuss the matter. Enclosed herewith for your reference only is the company's brochure.

Yours as ever,

Veronica Makepeace

for GOD

G:VM

DICTATED BUT NOT READ

UNIVERSAL CONSTRUCTION CO.
General Builders & Contractors

3rd Arch Along
Limepit Viaduct
Telephone 18194804612 (one line)
Telex CONU
MEMBER OF THE FEDERATION OF SMALL BUILDERS AND BUILDING CONTRACTORS

ar God,

Please find enclosed a number of suggestions for the world what drew up myself.

Yours sincerely,

Gwyn MacTaggart (Secretary)

Gwyn MacTaggart
Executive Secretary

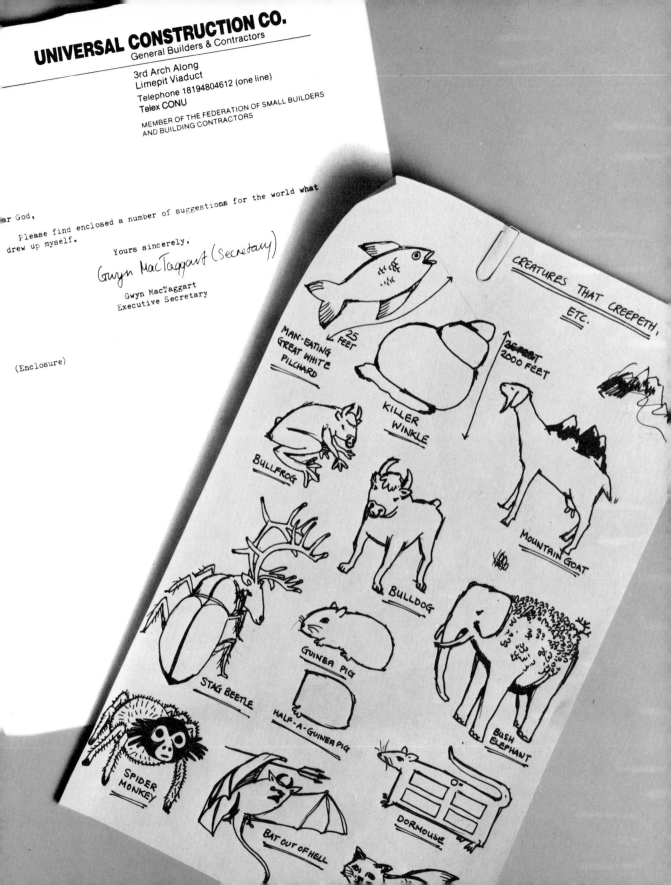

(Enclosure)

GRAVE-AN-IMAGE LTD

A member of the Widenberger Group of Companies

Imagine the scene. A new creation. A brand new world. It should be an enjoyable time; a time filled with happiness and thanksgiving. Yet all too often it's a time of sadness and regret. Why? Because not enough time has gone into the choice of the man to live in that world. Of course no one can be sure they've constructed exactly the right sort of man. But we like to think we've come as close as possible to *eliminating* all *avoidable* error, by listing all details of man on our computer. That means you get the man you want. Or something very close to it. Because we match your requirements to the men available.
With GRAVE-AN-IMAGE we guarantee to supply you with a suitable man for the job, or your money back. Just fill in the simple questionnaire below. And we'll supply you with a sample man by return.

JUST TICK THE ONE WHO MOST NEARLY MATCHES YOUR REQUIREMENTS

I would like the man to be:
- ☐ liken to me (please enclose photo)
- ☐ liken to someone else (please enclose someone else's photo)
- ☐ liken to Donny Osmond (please don't enclose photo)
- ☐ liken to Howard Hughes (please enclose wallet)
- ☐ liken to Randolph Hearst (please enclose lawyer)

His hair must be:
- ☐ black
- ☐ brown
- ☐ grey
- ☐ green
- ☐ machine-washable

His skin must be:
- ☐ wrinkled
- ☐ grey
- ☐ tanned
- ☐ machine-washable

His hobbies must be:
- ☐ football
- ☐ duckshooting
- ☐ macramé and embroidery
- ☐ speedway and other butch pursuits
- ☐ Spanish Military History 1680-1750

I would like his temperament to be:
- ☐ cool
- ☐ hot
- ☐ medium
- ☐ medium dry

I would like him to have:
- ☐ 1 leg
- ☐ 3 legs
- ☐ 17 legs

To GRAVE-AN-IMAGE LIMITED

Yes, I am interested in your services. Please rush me absolutely everything you've got on the subject even if it means you have to get up from your desk and open a drawer in your filing cabinet.

Name..

Age.................... **(please state alternative age)**....................

Address..

Where you hide your back door key..

COSMIC FINANCIAL CORPORATION

BIGGEST IN THE UNIVERSE

TELEPHONE:964359214 to 954359792 (inclusive)
TELEX:AMALWORLDS

Dear God:

Re: Creation of World

At last some reasonable news! The Board of Directors of Cosmic Financial have agreed to issue a provisional contract for the Creation of the World.

However, it was only brought about after much bending of the ear, and no less bending of the arm. I mention this because I fear that in the cold light of day there will be a good deal of recrimination and, perhaps, reconsideration.

The end result is that, in persuading the Board to go ahead, I have put myself in a pretty unenviable position. I must ask you to stress again to the builders that the work must be finished on time! And on budget!!

Perhaps when you write to the builders you could ask them to return the attached contract as soon as possible. All they need to do is sign on the dotted line. Assuming they can write, that is.

Yours as ever,

T.G. Cohen

T.G. COHEN
Project Development Officer

THIS IS
V.V.V.
IMPORTA

A Contract

* WRITE YOUR COMPANY'S NAME HERE

This contract is hereby issued on the .... day of .... between *........... .... and .... for the Creation (hereinafter referred to as "The Creation") of (hereinafter referred to as "of") the World (hereinafter referred to as "The World").

This contract shall refer and afford unto the said hereinafter persons all deed and trust as hereinbefore so ferred to. Terms as hereinsobefore listed.

PLEASE NOTE

The World shall comprise one large round object being of sound construction and design that shall revolve in a revolve-wise direction. This object shall be capable of spinning in an orbit around other objects, and shall be so constructed so that bits don't keep falling off and annoying people.

REMEMBER NO SMELLS

The World shall not make a grinding sound when it goes round. It mustn't smell either. It mustn't give out belching clouds of black smoke.

In construction of the aforementioned World hereinbefore referred to and hereinafter referred to, all work shall use specified materials.

e World shall be built in a period not
ceeding 7 (seven) days, including 1
ne) day's rest. If the period not
ceeding 7 (seven) days shall exceed
(seven) days, then a penalty clause
ereinafter referred to as "The Penalty
ause") shall be invoked which shall
reafter bring so to bear such penalties
be decreed fit by those who shall be
quired to determine such penalties.
particular, all penalties will be
dged by a panel of judges (herein-
ter referred to as "The Judgment
nel") who shall be so required to
dge all penalties.

) All time required to complete such work as shall be completed shall be recorded in a book, which shall be made fully available to any person wishing to inspect such records. Where such records are not required to be so inspected, then it shall not be necessary for a record to be produced. However, if someone changes their mind and says, "I think I'd rather like to see those records after all," then they shall be allowed so to do.

(2) Whereinsobefore and hereunto The World is completed, a deed stating that The World is complete shall be presented to any person or persons wishing to see such deed.

<u>Notes</u>

1. The notes which hereinafter shall be referred to as "The Notes."
2. No other notes shall be allowed to be called "The Notes."
3. No other part of this document shall be referred to as "The Notes."

A special pamphlet entitled "Where to Find The Notes" shall be supplied as an appendix to this document.

5. There are no more Notes after this one.

This document is witnessed and sealed on the ..... day of ....
between .... and ....
....
(Witness) (Witness)

"God"

Dear Mr. Scrummage,

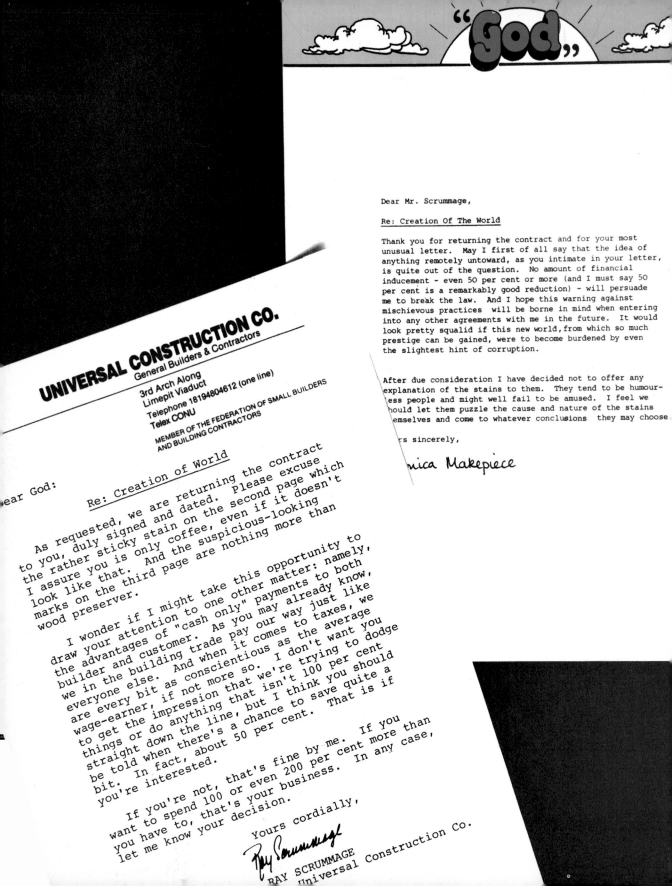

Re: Creation Of The World

Thank you for returning the contract and for your most unusual letter. May I first of all say that the idea of anything remotely untoward, as you intimate in your letter, is quite out of the question. No amount of financial inducement - even 50 per cent or more (and I must say 50 per cent is a remarkably good reduction) - will persuade me to break the law. And I hope this warning against mischievous practices will be borne in mind when entering into any other agreements with me in the future. It would look pretty squalid if this new world, from which so much prestige can be gained, were to become burdened by even the slightest hint of corruption.

After due consideration I have decided not to offer any explanation of the stains to them. They tend to be humour-less people and might well fail to be amused. I feel we hould let them puzzle the cause and nature of the stains emselves and come to whatever conclusions they may choose.

rs sincerely,

nica Makepiece

UNIVERSAL CONSTRUCTION CO.
General Builders & Contractors

3rd Arch Along
Limepit Viaduct
Telephone 18194804612 (one line)
Telex CONU

MEMBER OF THE FEDERATION OF SMALL BUILDERS AND BUILDING CONTRACTORS

ear God:

Re: Creation of World

As requested, we are returning the contract to you, duly signed and dated. Please excuse the rather sticky stain on the second page which I assure you is only coffee, even if it doesn't look like that. And the suspicious-looking marks on the third page are nothing more than wood preserver.

I wonder if I might take this opportunity to draw your attention to one other matter: namely the advantages of "cash only" payments to both builder and customer. As you may already know, we in the building trade pay our way just like everyone else. And when it comes to taxes, we are every bit as conscientious as the average wage-earner, if not more so. I don't want you to get the impression that we're trying to dodge things or do anything that isn't 100 per cent straight down the line, but I think you should be told when there's a chance to save quite a bit. In fact, about 50 per cent. That is if you're interested.

If you're not, that's fine by me. If you want to spend 100 or even 200 per cent more than you have to, that's your business. In any case, let me know your decision.

Yours cordially,

Ray Scrummage

RAY SCRUMMAGE
Universal Construction Co.

COSMIC FINANCIAL CORPORATION

BIGGEST IN THE UNIVERSE

TELEPHONE:964359214 to 954359792 (inclusive)
TELEX:AMALWORLDS

Dear Sirs(s):

<u>Creation of the World</u>

My underling, T.G. Cohen, has suggested that I might drop you a line in my capacity as Managing Director of Cosmic Financial Corporation to tell you how pleased we are that the above project has gotten off the ground (although it's about time). It is with very great pleasure that I can allow you to thank me for permitting you to embark upon this project.

It is a project that I trust you will carry out to the best of your abilities and which my staff will be glad to help you with in any way possible.

I hope that you will enjoy working with Cosmic Financial Corporation.

With my best wishes,

R.V. Goldenstein

R.V. GOLDENSTEIN (Mrs.)
Managing Director

"God,"

Dear Mr. Cohen

Re: Creation Of The World

Thank you for all your recent letters. Please tell Mrs Goldenstein that I am equally pleased that the project is now under way.

I continue to receive letters of advice from many authorities which I believe may be of interest. When you have had a chance to study them, perhaps you would return them to me, together with any comments.

Yours sincerely,

Veronica Makepiece

Contagious Dis

INCORPORATING UNITED COUGHS, CONSOLIDATED WHEEZES AND UNIVERSAL ILLNESS

Dear God,

Thank you for your letter requesting our prices for supplying assorted diseases.

However, we very much regret that, following an unfortunate incident involving a fragile test tube, a highly contagious substance and a solid stone floor, the staff here have fallen victim to a particularly virulent attack of pestilence, and are at present unable to offer any help.

However, if you are willing to call round to our offices and stand by an open window, then I feel sure we could supply you with any diseases you might require.

Yours contagiously,

Stanley Goodwin

Stanley Goodwin
Sales Department

---

rainy days

SUPPLIERS OF CLIMATE, WEATHER AND ASSORTED METEOROLOGY

My dear God,

Re: Creation of The World

Please find enclosed a sample of the climates we now have in stock. We would confirm our prices as follows:

Polar Climate	Includes ice, snow, wind, rain, sleet, plus 240-page operating manual $155.00
Temperate Climate	Includes ice, snow, wind, rain, sleet, and one day of sunshine $225.00
Tropical Climate	Includes sun, sun, and isolated showers (optional extras include monsoon, typhoons, hurricanes and snow) $330.00
Equatorial Climate	Includes sun, sun, and sun (optional extras include sunglasses) $960.00

Yours sincerely,

Seamus MacIntosh.

Seamus MacIntosh
For Rainy Days

MARSH LANDS

EVERYTHING FOR YOUR BOG

Dear God:

Thank you for your letter inquiring about our line of marshes and swamps. Our standard range consists of:

> <u>Junior Swamp</u> 4' x 6' with clip-on fixing. Can be rolled up and put away when not required.
> <u>Economy Swamp</u> A tough, rugged swamp with extruded rubber foliage that needs no maintenance. Fits any space.
> <u>Jumbo Swamp</u> Special large size swamp with lots of large chunky weeds and thick grass. Will not fray around the edges.

In addition to the above, we have recently started to market 3' x 2' swamp floor tiles. Each tile is made from a tough, rugged, grasslike material and is foam backed for extra hard wearing. Each tile can be lifted and replaced when necessary.

May we draw your attention to one minor point: the need for correct installation. Incorrectly installed swamps will fray and crack and produce unsightly damp patches along adjoining vegetation.

Yours sincerely,

Clifford Sniggling

Clifford Sniggling

GEOLOGICAL FEATURES

Dear God,

Thank you for your letter. We do indeed stock geological features suitable for new worlds. You may care to visit our showrooms and inspect the full range of products available.

Of particular interest to your current needs would be our extensive range of monoclinal shifting (lateral erosional activity taking place where a river flows along the strike of a gently dipping rock strata and a less resistant stratum overlies one or more resistances). These are always very popular with amateur creators and no world is complete without one.

I would also like to draw your attention to our superb range of igneous intrusions which are ideal for all climates and are suitable for indoor and outdoor use.

Yours sincerely,

Norman Turgid

Norman Turgid

<u>Sales Officer</u>

“God”

Dear Mr. Scrummage:

Re: Creation Of The World

Thank you for your letter. I am sure you will understand me when I say that I was more than a little concerned by its content. As you will recall, we had made a firm commitment to a mutally acceptable starting date, so it has come as something of a shock for me to learn that you now wish that date to be rearranged.

I am sure you do indeed have "other things going" and that it would be difficult to fit in the required work. But I must point out that we all have other commitments and the totally selfish attitude you exhibit is not one I applaud. Nor, incidentally, do I approve of you referring to me as "chief".

I am someone who prides himself on humility and I am therefore reluctant to start throwing my weight around at this juncture. However, be warned that I am not at all pleased with this setback and I trust you will take every step to ensure it does not happen again.

Yours insistently,

Veronica Makepiece

for GOD

G:VM

DICTATED BUT NOT READ

Dear Mr. Scrummage,

Re: Creation Of The World

Your latest letter has just reached me. Might I suggest that in the future you invest in a postage stamp; from a purely personal point of view, I always find it achieves a faster reaction from the postman.

Thank you for letting me know your plans for a new date on which to start the creation. I am sure a week from Tuesday will be acceptable to us. We had rather hoped that work might start on Monday and finish on Sunday. We felt that this would look better in the history books, but as time is short we are prepared to forego this academic nicety.

Sincerely,

Veronica Makepiece

for God

Re: Creation of The World

My secretary has just passed to me a letter which she begged I did not read in front of her. I can see why. The contents caused me to quite lose control and, had the poor girl been present, I fear I might indeed have beaten her senseless in my raging fury.

Yes, you are quite right to suppose I wouldn't be at all pleased to learn you can't make Tuesday. And yes, I do consider a long-standing customer's leaking guttering insufficient excuse for your not being able to attend. What is guttering in comparison with the creation of a world? And no, I certainly won't accept your abject apologies.

You are, I am sure, fully aware that Amalgamated Worlds are an extremely large and important company and that the repercussions resulting from our letting them down are likely to be enormous. I for my part see no reason why any of the blame should attach itself to me. You may therefore be assured that when the proverbial hits the fan - as it inevita will - it will be you and not me who faces the wrath of those concerned.

I trust that in this light of this advice you will now reconsider your decision.

Yours forcefully,

Veronica Makepiece

pp. God

"God"

Dear Mr. Scrummage:

Re: Creation Of The World

Your latest letter reached me today and I must confess that I am still far from happy. Thursday may be 'only two days late' to you, but it represents a considerable delay on the original starting date.

However, it is at least (I would now assume) a definite date. I would far rather work to a schedule which can be relied upon than some fanciful date you have chosen using your calendar and a pin. I am therefore forced to accept your revised schedule. Reluctantly.

I must stress, however, that this new starting date must be kept at all costs. I will risk considerable scorn in presenting it to Cosmic Financial. You will risk far more if you fail to keep it.

Yours,

Veronica Makepiece
for GOD

G:VM

DICTATED BUT NOT READ

"God"

Dear Mr. Scrummage:

Re: Creation Of The World

I have spent the last ten minutes regaining my usual composure and tidying up a trail of total devastation.

After all that was said and written, I find it totally impossible to conceive how you could have the brass to consider asking for more time.

We are fearfully late! We are incurring the wrath of Cosmic Financial Corporation! We are about to embark upon perhaps the most memorable project ever! And all you can think about is some sordid little plan to defraud the taxman!!!!

Quite apart from everything else, it will now mean we start work on Sunday - the one day we had hoped to keep free as a day of rest. I can only suggest you write back immediately reconsidering the time schedule, or else start considering yourselves summarily dismissed.

Yours most aggrievedly,

Veronica Makepiece
for GOD

G:VM

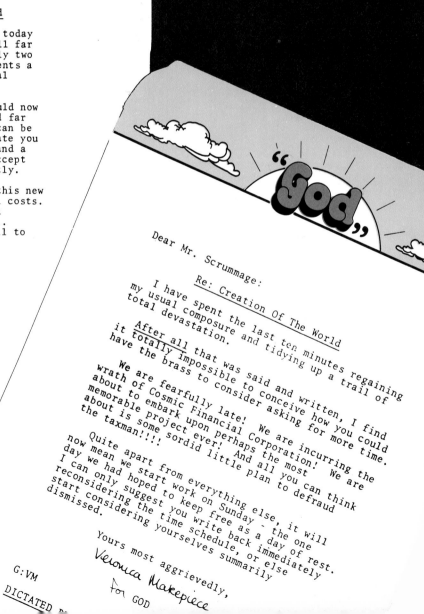

DICTATED B

Universal Franchises

Specialists in:

Mufflers
Chicken (fried, boiled, broasted)
Tacos
Burgers
Frankfurters and fries
Ice Cream
Softee Ice Cream
Slaves (only when licensed by local government)

Dear God,

We have heard about your fabulous "World" you are about to build. We wondered if you have given any thought to the financial advantages of Franchising.

If you don't understand Franchising, don't let it worry you. We understand it. Our accountants understand it even better than we do.

Although we can understand the creative pride you have or will have in your world, we should to point out that the really Big Bucks lie in efficiency of Mass Merchandising through multiple units.

Please call for further details.

Col. O. Julius Sanders

Col. O. Julius Sanders

"God"

Dear Mr. Cohen

Re: Creation Of The World

It is with regret that I have to inform you that we still await confirmation of a definite starting date from the builders. I can only apologise for this and trust that you will bear with me for just a trifle longer. I am hoping to receive further information within the next few days and will, of course, be in touch as soon as I have some news.

In the meantime, I thought you might like to see copies of some of the information I have received recently from suppliers regarding fixtures and fittings for the world. I am also enclosing copies of the letters I received from the Office of Patents and the Consolidated National Insurance Office, which I am sure you will find of particular interest.

Perhaps you would care to read through the enclosed and let me have your comments.

Yours sincerely,

Tanya Starr

PP. God

OFFICE OF PATENTS*

*Patent applied for

Dear Sir:

Thank you for your letter. From the information which you have supplied, I would make the following points:

> It would not be possible to patent the concept of the world per se. As you know, a large number of planets already exist and the idea of a new planet, or even a new galaxy, could at no time be construed to be sufficiently unique as to afford it patent status.

Yours faithfully,

Alison Kalahari

ALISON KALAHARI
Library

BODYSNATC

Skulls, mandibles, ribs (m. and f.), sternums, vert

CHIP RESISTANT! HEAT RESI

SELF-ADHESIVE BODY HAIR

Ideal for Italians

Pelvic Girdles

(discontinued line)

Huge reduction. For a new, slimmer you

(Can be fitted in under 5 minutes! Needs no washers!)

HANDS

$2 each or 3 for $5 (fingernails and tattoos extra)

SPINAL COLUMNS

with new rubberised flanges, vulcanised sprockets and high-tension intervertebral discs

(Contains no artificial ingredients)

RIBS

Buy direct from us at well below shop prices

SOLID CAST IRON

Skulls

Tough and rugged

'Award-winning Design'

CLIP-ON

Hernias – Add a touch of elegance to th
body with a strangulated hernia. Ma
styles available.

Noses

Choice of shapes

Greek, Roman, Bugner, Manilow

Please state whether stick-on, bolt-on, screw-on or glue-on fixings required

GALL BLADDERS

New special features include:

* stores digestive fluid secreted by the liver
* acts as reservoir for bile

Guaranteed against biliary colic

SNAP-ON FITMENT

Large quantity of warts — slightly damaged but will repair!

All shapes!
All colours!
All conditions!

ODDMENTS FOR SALE OR RENT

HAMSTRINGS Larynx, muscles, pelvis, tongue, ear, prostate. Must sell. Owner going abroad. First to see will buy.

ABDOMENS Please state preferred shape. Ideal for women and men. Also ideal for sheep, cows, hedgehogs.

HERS LTD

olumns, sacrums, scrotums (m. and f.)

T! RUST RESISTANT!

TEETH

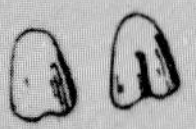

All sizes, all shapes
New and secondhand
new and reconditioned gums
ours: White, yellow, green, red, natural, tan

Feet

es
xus
oids
tory

Many unusual features:
Tibion avicullars
Collateral ligaments
Plantar ligaments
Corns
Please state whether left or right required

MOUTHS

Don't be confused by imitations! We stock the largest range of mouths. (Tongues not included)

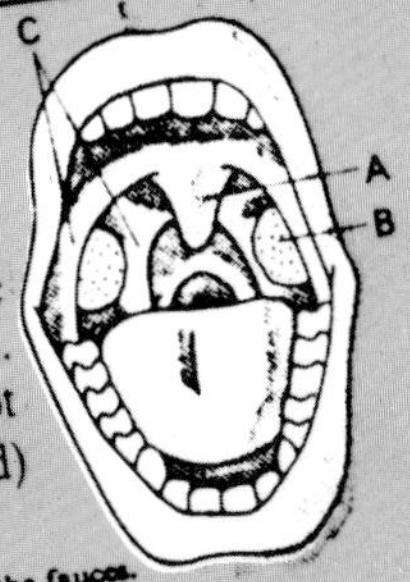

A. Uvula.
B. Tonsil.
C. Pillars of the fauces.

LYMPHATIC SYSTEMS AND SPLEENS

(Large quantity – slightly shop soiled but otherwise all right)
Ideal for first-time buyer

BRAINS ☆

Add that touch of luxury with a fully-fitted brain! Available in four sizes: small, medium, large, swotty.

Fits all leading makes of head.

Includes * olfactory bulb
* optic nerve
* cerebrum
* medulla
* cerebellum
* screws and washers

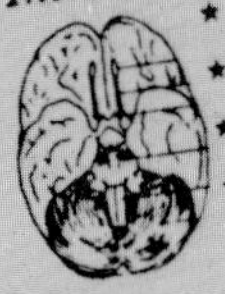

SKIN

Red, white, brown, yellow, black, pink and ash-grey available

Free estimate
Free fixing and fitting
Free underlay and sebaceous glands

ALIMENTARY CANAL

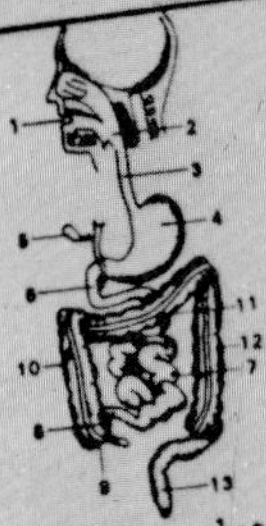

Fits Male and Female
Ideal for all digestive work
Non-regurgitative!
Ulcer-proof!

Complete with pharynx, oesophagus, stomach, gall bladder, duodenum, small intestine, colon (ileo-caecal valve extra)

f realism with an **IN-TOENAIL.** Fits any le.

ARY CANAL Only one owner from new. No offer accepted.

CH'S PLEXUS Only alec owner from new.

S TENDON Needs at-'ould suit jogger.

BLADDER Immaculate condition throughout. Full maintenance history available. Genuine reason for sale.

ULCERS Retired businessman has ulcers for sale. Would suit middle-aged, overworked, neurotic wreck.

Due to unforeseen objects I have a large number of **CUTS AND BRUISES** for sale. Please state quality and quantity when ordering. Ideal for insurance claims.

Choice of finishes: Bone, wood, plastic cardboard or chipboard

Eden's Garden Centre

Wild flowers • Trees
Wild fruits • Grasses • Ferns
Rushes • Fungi

FLOWERS
Marsh grass
Marsh weed
Marsh marigold
Marsh mallow
Deadly nightshade
Deadly lampshade
Pansy
Wild pansy
Absolutely livid pansy
Adder

TREES
Horse chestnut
Sweet chestnut
Man-eating chestnut
Lombardy poplar
Ford poplar
Ford poplar 1300E
Giant redwood
Giant redhead
Beech
Palm beech
Yew *(Taxus baccata)*

MUSHROOMS
Bleeding agaric
Bleeding morel
Morel support
Death cap
Shaggy cap

RUSHES
Common rush
Hard rush
Round fruited rush
Toad rush
Bulrush
Mad rush

REG AND WARREN BILBOUS

Vegetation Supplies (Trade Only)

NOW AVAILABLE

Tundra
A very cold, very dull, very icy type of climate. Good for those who like very cold, dull, icy types of climate.

Coniferous Forests
Quite cold, quite dull, quite icy ... but with trees. Ideal for tree-fetishists who can't resist the firm young boughs of supple young pine trees as they twist and bend erotically in the wind.

Broad-leaved Forests
Not quite so cold or as icy as above. But still pretty dull. Ideal for deep-water fish who like broad-leaved trees.

Mediterranean Vegetation
Quite nice and pleasant, with lots of vines and sycamores and things like that. Especially ideal for people called Guiseppi and Giovanni ... and things like that.

BEASTS

Exotic! Unusual! Bizarre! Cheap!

Suppliers of exotic wildlife, exotic wildlife meat pies, exotic wildlife pastries, exotic wildlife cut into bite-sized peices and placed in a saucepan with onions, milk, water and seasoning (serves 4-6).

The following are available for immediate delivery:

Animals

Hedgehog
Mole
Common shrew
Uncommon shrew
Common weasel
Common badger
Otter
Skunk
Ferret
Polecat
Brown hare
Short hare
Body hare
Flying squirrel
Black rat
Grey rat
Common rat
Dirty rat
Dormouse
Dorbell
Harvest mouse
Harvest moose
Chocolate moose
Blue whale
Killer whale
Flying whale

Birds

Blackbird
Bullfinch
Great bustard
Rotten bustard
Golden eagle
Golden beagle
Golden seagull
Peregrine falcon
Peregrine sparrow
Mallard
Goose
Lesser spotted goose
Rook
Hedge sparrow
House sparrow
Wheel sparrow
Pigeon
Barn owl
Eagle owl
Stormy petrel
Pheasant
Black tern
Sooty tern
Little tern
Great tit
Blue tit
Bearded tit
Bearded tit with a sexual identity crisis
Robin redtit
Vulture

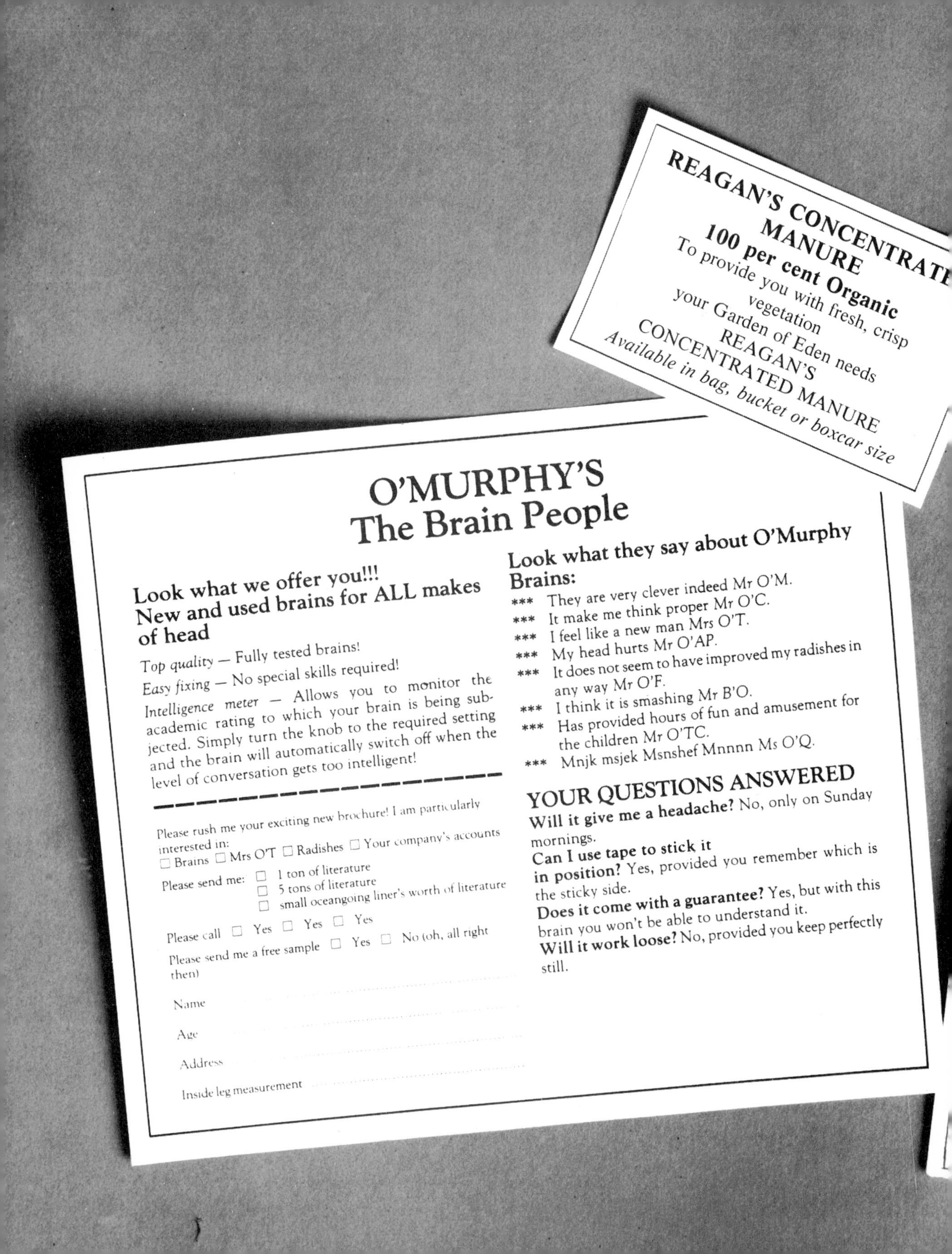

REAGAN'S CONCENTRATE
MANURE
100 per cent Organic
To provide you with fresh, crisp vegetation
your Garden of Eden needs
REAGAN'S
CONCENTRATED MANURE
Available in bag, bucket or boxcar size

O'MURPHY'S
The Brain People

Look what we offer you!!! New and used brains for ALL makes of head

Top quality — Fully tested brains!

Easy fixing — No special skills required!

Intelligence meter — Allows you to monitor the academic rating to which your brain is being sub- jected. Simply turn the knob to the required setting and the brain will automatically switch off when the level of conversation gets too intelligent!

Please rush me your exciting new brochure! I am particularly interested in:
☐ Brains ☐ Mrs O'T ☐ Radishes ☐ Your company's accounts

Please send me: ☐ 1 ton of literature
☐ 5 tons of literature
☐ small oceangoing liner's worth of literature

Please call ☐ Yes ☐ Yes ☐ Yes

Please send me a free sample ☐ Yes ☐ No (oh, all right then)

Name ....

Age ....

Address ....

Inside leg measurement ....

Look what they say about O'Murphy Brains:

*** They are very clever indeed Mr O'M.
*** It make me think proper Mr O'C.
*** I feel like a new man Mrs O'T.
*** My head hurts Mr O'AP.
*** It does not seem to have improved my radishes in any way Mr O'F.
*** I think it is smashing Mr B'O.
*** Has provided hours of fun and amusement for the children Mr O'TC.
*** Mnjk msjek Msnshef Mnnnn Ms O'Q.

YOUR QUESTIONS ANSWERED

Will it give me a headache? No, only on Sunday mornings.

Can I use tape to stick it in position? Yes, provided you remember which is the sticky side.

Does it come with a guarantee? Yes, but with this brain you won't be able to understand it.

Will it work loose? No, provided you keep perfectly still.

Creating a world can be time-consuming and ifficult. However, Frankenstein's can help hen you have more expensive things to buy, ke a [redacted] and a Swedish [redacted] th [redacted] like melons, and who knows a od time when she sees one!

Contact your nearest Frankenstein's agent, or pop into one of our regional offices. Because when you create, we don't.

FRANKENSTEIN'S

An im

THE ROYA
STRICTLY LIMITED ED

'This is .

The Royal House of MacLozenge, in conjunction with Massive Rip Offs Ltd., are very, very proud to announce a very, very unique offer: the COUNTRIES OF THE WORLD Limited Edition Set. These are not models or miniatures. They are full-size, fully working countries that you can add to your world. And now, for a very, very limited period, we are able to offer subscribers the chance to purchase a complete, marked, signed set of these countries.

Each country when placed in a prominent position in your world will create a most impressive feature that will cause your guests and friends to exclaim 'Ooh', 'Ah' and 'Cor, I wish those countries were mine'. Not only that, but you can use them in the confidence that they will not scratch, chip, fade or rust.

Imagine the pleasure and pride of owning this truly remarkable collection. A collection that is sure to appreciate in value. Overnight. In fact, most sets appreciate in value in a matter of seconds. Why, even in the short period since you began to read this advertisement, you can bet some lucky blighter has profited by three or four hundred per cent just because he was sensible enough to invest in COUNTRIES OF THE WORLD. In fact, you'd be stupid not to rush out straight away and post off your application form. Ab-

solutely mac
for your set
in anguish ju
fer it is.

Each cour
craftsman wc
light, with no
wage. Which
our ridiculous
what we were
was so shocke
told him the p
heart attack a

This is the or
this Special Ed
may be offere
decide to keep
tunities to subsc
ched things. T
limited to the tc

All countries
shown. The shap
are different to
honest, they're n
in any way.

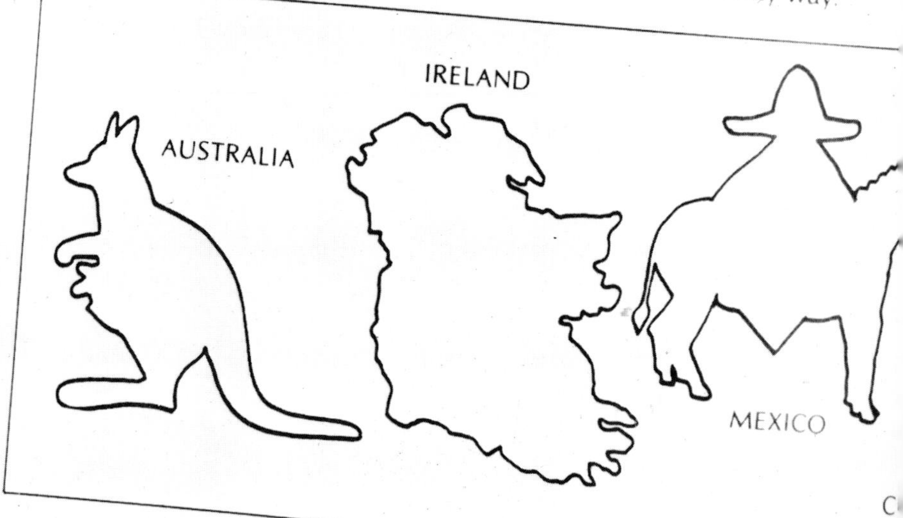

: announcement for creators:

OUSE OF MacLOZENGE
N OF COUNTRIES OF THE WORLD

e opportunity for collectors'

be so stupid if you didn't send off
uld literally tear off my own head
k about it. That's how good an of-

been uniquely crafted by a true
least 26 hours a day in appalling
dustrial clothing, and at a pitiful
son why we can offer the set at
rice. Indeed, when I first heard
ask for a set of these countries I
to see the doctor. And when I
vas so shocked he had a mild
retire from general practice.
tunity you will have to acquire
course, a further opportunity
ter date. And we might just
ring more and more oppor-
il we've got rid of all the wret-
otal edition will be strictly
er we sell.
led at a different size to that
fferent, too. And the names
hown here. In fact, let's be
ly like the ones shown here

ORDER FORM COUNTRIES OF THE WORLD

Please enter my order for Countries of the World. I enclose herewith a blank cheque made out to Massive Rip Offs Ltd. I understand that in the future I will pay you vast sums of money. And I understand that, even when I think you've finally stopped making demands for cash, you will still call round and ask me for jewellery and the family silver. I also understand that if I don't give you what you want then you will hit me over the head. I will receive an invoice within a few days and another one a few days after that. I will then receive more invoices. Then the invoices will stop and the threatening letters will begin. I shall of course be given the opportunity to cough up first. Or else you'll come round and shoot off my kneecaps, poke out my eyes, and break both my arms.

Signature (USE BLOCK CAPITALS) ____________

Name ____________

Address ____________

____

____

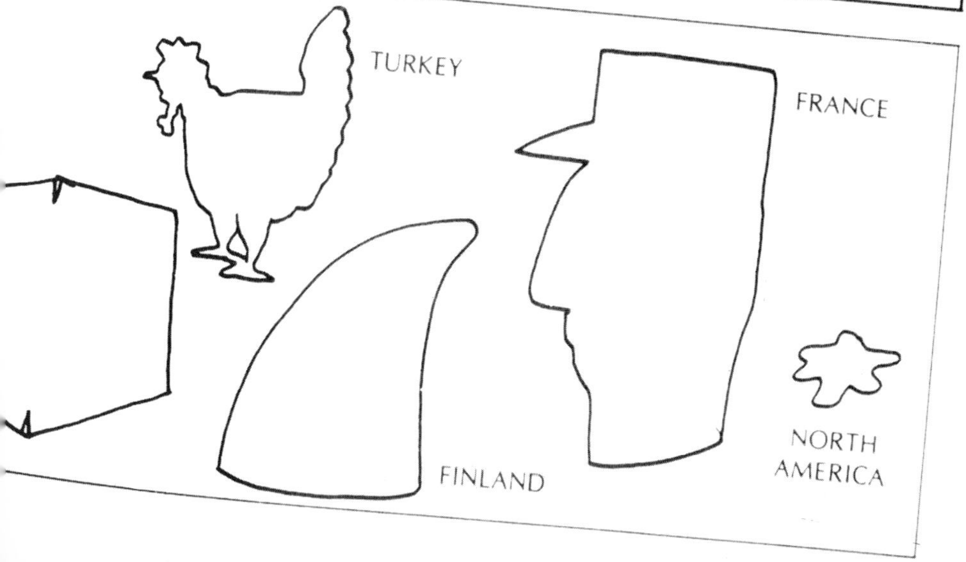

COSMIC FINANCIAL CORPORATION

BIGGEST IN THE UNIVERSE

TELEPHONE:964359214 to 954359792 (inclusive)
TELEX:AMALWORLDS

Dear God:

Re: Creation of World

Many thanks for sending me all the information about supplies for the world. You certainly seem to have been busy, but I notice that you've been keeping rather quiet about next Sunday's starting date.

Perhaps you could drop me a quick line just to confirm that all is proceeding as planned.

With very best wishes,

T.G. Cohen

T.G. COHEN
Project Development Officer

"God"

Dear Mr. Scrummage:

Re: Creation of The World

May I point out that I am still awaiting confirmation that you are ready to start work next Sunday.

Yours concernedly,

Veronica Makepiece
for GOD

G:VM

DICTATED BUT NOT READ

SHUSTER, SHYSTER, SUSHI, and POLLOCK

Attorneys at Law

Dear Mr. Stagworthy,

Re: Creation Of The World

We act as attorneys for Mr. God, who has asked that we contact you with regard to the above-named project for which I believe your firm has been contracted as builders.

Mr. God is considerably alarmed at the breach of contract - a contract to which, I may add, you were a signatory - and which gives reference to all conditions relating to the hereinsobeforementioned subject. And, indeed, it would appear from all discussions which have taken place that you are in flagrant breach of this contract and that legally you are in an invidious positior

Mr. God fears that a legal settlement of the issue may be the only solution now available to him, and he has suggested we write to you to point this out and to urge that you reconsider your position in the matter.

As it is not our normal practice to offer free legal advice to our clients' adversaries. However, in this instance we make exception to this, if only to impress upon you the utter hopelessness of the position you are now in. We would suggest that without delay you re-examine all aspects of this issue and consider whether you cannot offer a suitable response.

In particular, we would draw your attention to:

1. Your reference to possible fraudulent practice in the offer of low prices in return for cash settlements for work done.
2. The unnatural practices and behavior called for in your specifications and worksheets that would appear to contravene health and safety requirements.
3. Your continued failure to begin work, and your flagrant breach of agreements made as to the timing of such work.

May I therefore expect your immediate reply.

Yours Legally,

P.P. Scribbling

P.P. Scribbling (Partner)

UNIVERSAL CONSTRUCTION CO.

General Builders & Contractors

3rd Arch Along
Limepit Viaduct
Telephone 18194804612 (one line)
Telex CONU

MEMBER OF THE FEDERATION OF SMALL BUILDERS AND BUILDING CONTRACTORS

God:

Creation of The World

ust inform you that our colleague, Mr. cummage, is no longer with us, since an fortunate misunderstanding with the IRS s necessitated his leaving our employ ather hurriedly. I must stress that in no ay was our firm implicated, and that the ncident involved some "extra" work Mr. crummage had undertaken on his own time.

As a result of Mr. Scrummage's hasty departure I am assuming responsibility for all his work. I regret I was not acquainted with your particular case until now, and was concerned on opening your file to see that a certain amount of friction has occurred. For the moment I must beg you to bear with me. I must therefore warn you that the Sunday date does seem highly unlikely. In two or three weeks we will have a much clearer idea where we stand and I will contact you then to report further.

Yours soothingly,

Ted Slagworthy

TED SLAGWORTHY
versal Construction Co.

UNIVERSAL CONSTRUCTION CO.
General Builders & Contractors

3rd Arch Along
Limepit Viaduct
Telephone 18194804612 (one line)
Telex CONU

MEMBER OF THE FEDERATION OF SMALL BUILDERS AND BUILDING CONTRACTORS

Dear God,

Re: Creation of The World

I have just received the letter from your attorney, and confess I was somewhat upset by its tone. I did assure you we are making every effort to attend to your work, and I had hoped you would not feel it necessary to employ an attorney to this end.

I am now in the process of working through our order book and would anticipate starting work on your world four weeks from today. Perhaps you would let me know if that would be convenient for you.

Yours huffily,

Gwyn MacTaggart (Secretary)
Ted Slagworthy
Universal Construction Co.

"God"

Dear Mr. Slagworthy:

Re: Creation Of The World

Four weeks is totally out of the question! This work should have been finished weeks ago. I am already in the embarrassing position of having to approach Cosmic Financial Corporation and say that the work has yet to be started.

You'd better rethink your position.

Yours crossly,

Veronica Makepeace
For GOD

G:VM

DICTATED BUT NOT READ

SHUSTER, SHYSTER, SUSHI, and POLLOCK

Attorneys at Law

Dear Mr. Slagworthy,

Re: Creation of the World

Once again Mr. God has asked that I write to you about the breach of the contract to which you were a signatory. He has asked me to point out that, if you are not prepared to reconsider your position in the matter, he will have no option but to instruct us to serve notice that we intend to sue.

I trust you will therefore assume from this letter that Mr. God is no longer prepared to tolerate delay and is now taking legal advice with regard to court proceedings. I would be grateful if on receipt of this letter you would contact my office to discuss your considered position. Failure to do so will be assumed to imply your continued intransigence and notice will therefore be served upon you.

Yours accusingly,

P.P. Scribbling

P.P. Scribbling (Partner)

Telephone Message

TIME RECEIVED 3·30pm. DATE

FROM UNIV. CONST. CO.

MR. SLAGWORTHY PHONED WHILE YOU WERE OUT. APOLOGISED BUT NO CHANCE OF ALTERING THE DATE.
ASKED HIM IF THERE WAS ANY OTHER NEWS BUT PHONE WENT DEAD BEFORE HE COULD REPLY. ASSUME HE RAN OUT OF COINS.

RECEIVED BY V.

UNIVERSAL CONSTRUCTION CO.
General Builders & Contractors

3rd Arch Along
Limepit Viaduct
Telephone 18194804612 (one line)
Telex CONU

MEMBER OF THE FEDERATION OF SMALL BUILDERS AND BUILDING CONTRACTORS

Dear God:

I was very disappointed to receive another letter from your attorney regarding the starting date for the creation of the world. As you will realize, the building trade is of necessity somewhat flexible, and to be held to strict dates and schedules is irksome and impractical and does no one any good.

I hope you will be patient. Quite apart from the fact that we are now under-staffed, we have another big job which should have been completed last year. After that a couple of garages to be built. Then you.

I will write again just as soon as possible.

Yours sincerely,

Gwyn MacTaggart (Secretary)

GWYN MACTAGGART

123498 CONU G

112 GOD G

ATTN: TED SLAGWORTHY

LATEST LETTER TOTALLY UNACCEPTABLE. QUITE ESSENTIAL THAT WORLD BE STARTED WITHIN WEEK. CANNOT KEEP COSMIC FINANCIAL WAITING ANY LONGER AND FEAR MY STANDING WITH THEM WILL BE SEVERELY ERODED UNLESS I CAN OFFER IMMEDIATE SATISFACTION.

GOD

Telephone Message

DATE

TIME RECEIVED 2.30pm

FROM UNIV. CONST. CO.

MR. SLAGWORTHY (UNIVERSAL) PHONED WHILE YOU WERE OUT AT THE OSTEOPATH. HAS RECEIVED YOUR TELEX. WILL START TWO WEEKS FROM WEDNESDAY.

RECEIVED BY Veronica

123498 CONU G
112 GOD G

ATTN: TED SLAGWORTHY

TWO WEEKS FROM WEDNESDAY NOT ACCEPTABLE.
EARLIER DATE OR WILL SEEK ALTERNATIVE
BUILDER IN ADDITION TO FILING LAWSUIT.
REPLY REQUIRED IMMEDIATEST.

GOD

Telephone Message

TIME RECEIVED 3.30pm DATE

FROM UNIV. CONST. CO.

MR. SLAGWORTHY PHONED WHILE
YOU WERE OUT AT THE CHEMIST'S
GETTING OSTEOPATH'S PRESCRIPTION.
RECEIVED LATEST TELEX. SUGGEST
WEEK FROM TUESDAY INSTEAD.

RECEIVED BY Veronica

Telephone Messa

TIME RECEIVED 3.35pm. DATE

FROM OSTEOPATH

OSTEOPATH PHONED!
MOST IMPORTANT - HE GAV
WRONG PRESCRIPTION! ON NO AC
USE LINAMENT! EFFECTS UNKN
MEANT FOR CATTLE! PLEASE C
NEW PRESCR

RECEIVED BY Veronica

ATTN: TED SLAGWORTHY

WEEK FROM MONDAY LATEST POSSIBLE DATE THAT
CAN BE ACCEPTED.

GOD

Telephone Message

TIME RECEIVED 4.30pm. DATE

FROM UNIV. CONST. CO.

MR. SLAGWORTHY PHONED...
RELUCTANT, BUT ACCEPT DATE!
WILL START MONDAY WEEK.

RECEIVED BY Veronica

Veronica
Would you please place the attached adertisement in a prominent position in the ~~revelant~~ relevant trade journals and ring the estate agent with a view to locating more sizeable office accommodation than this place.
Have just popped out to the sweet shop
G

Dear Sir or Madam,

I am 36, highly intelligent, suave, incredibly attractive, smartly dressed and extremely modest. I would like to be considered for your

Dear Sir or Madam,

I am a 16-year-old schoolgirl and would like to be considered for the position of Person Friday for your

Dear Sir,

Creation of the World

I am an 83-year-old schoolgirl and I would be like to be considered for the position of Person Friday for the above

Dear Sirs,

Re: Your Advertisement

I was an 83-year-old schoolgirl until I discovered genetic engineering. Now I am an 83-year-old wombat called Terry and

r Sir,

Re: Creation Of The World (Person Friday)

I wonder if you would be prepared to consider me for the above position. I have been interested in Creation for a number of years, and have myself done a considerable amount of research into animal and plant anatomy.

I have my own chain saw and mallet together with a twelve bore

CREATION OF A WORLD PROJECT
VACANCY FOR A
PERSON FRIDAY

Due to pressure of work, a Person Friday is urgently required for this hectic but exciting office. Duties will include filing, operating telex, some typing, making coffee (with and without sugar), keeping an appointment list, sealing and stamping all letters, and running office when other staff are away.

The suitable applicant will be loving, warm, gentle, sharp (but able to forgive), rough, tough, sincere (without being ingratiating), debonair, brave, literate, and into astrology, health foods and all kinds of music.

Previous experience would be useful. The applicant should have a clean driving record and a positive desire to see new worlds created.

Please apply Box No. 746712.5 enclosing a current curriculum vitae.

Dear Sir:

PERSON FRIDAY VACANCY

I wonder if you would be willing to consider me for your position for Person Friday. I am tall, blonde, good looking, and have this incredible sexy body that just turns men on. My name is Michael.

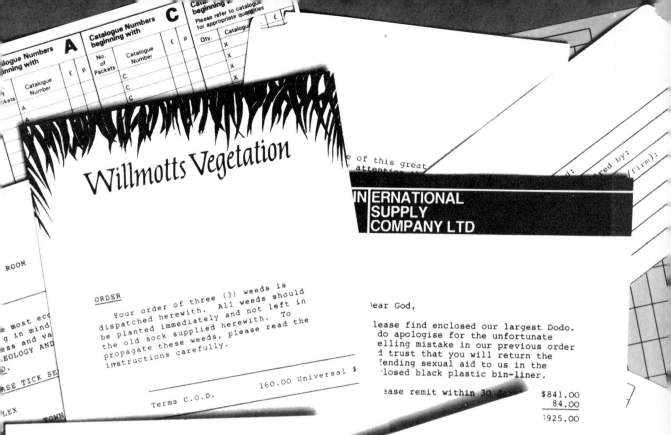

	Catalogue Numbers beginning with A				Catalogue Numbers beginning with C				Catalogue Numbers beginning with ...
No. of Packets	Catalogue Number	£	p	No. of Packets	Catalogue Number	£	p	Qty.	Catalogue
	A				C				X
	A				C				X
					C				X

Please refer to catalogue for appropriate quantities

Willmotts Vegetation

ORDER

Your order of three (3) weeds is dispatched herewith. All weeds should be planted immediately and not left in the old sock supplied herewith. To propagate these weeds, please read the instructions carefully.

160.00 Universal $

Terms C.O.D.

...e of this great
... attention ...

...INERNATIONAL SUPPLY COMPANY LTD

...ear God,

...lease find enclosed our largest Dodo.
... do apologise for the unfortunate
...elling mistake in our previous order
...d trust that you will return the
...fending sexual aid to us in the
...losed black plastic bin-liner.

...ease remit within 30 ...

	$841.00
	84.00
	...925.00

ROOM

...e most eco...
...g in mind...
...ess and va...
...EOLOGY AND...
...D.
...ASE TICK SE...
...LEX
TOWN...

ANIMALS OSCAR'S WILD ANIMALS

We supply herewith a selection from our range of Bengali Tigers. As you will no doubt appreciate, Bengali Tigers are not particularly easy things to pack and I'm afraid that in this case we had considerable trouble getting the wretched things to stay still long enough for us to tie the wrapping paper down. Might I suggest that in light of this you perhaps keep a weapon handy when unpacking.

Universal $

Terms strictly 7 days

TIGERS (three)	100.00
VET	58.00
Sales Tax	6.00
TOTAL:	164.00

THINGS ON EARTH

INVOICE

Please find herewith your order for 1 (one) skunk (medium/small). We suggest you don't open the airtight bag downwind, and as an added precaution you might like to consider employing someone with a heavy cold to do the job for you. Should you wish to return the skunk to us for any reason, would you please use a sealed plastic bag and mark the package 'SKUNK', otherwise it will upset the girls in our packaging department.

Terms (one month)

Skunk	$25.00
Airtight box	1.00
Second airtight box	1.00
Airtight bag	0.50
Sales Tax	3.00
TOTAL:	$30.50

...red by:
...(firm):
...etrol

ATTN: TED SLAGWORTHY
TUESDAY 10.00 A.M.

AM FRANKLY APPALLED TO FIND NO WORK BEGUN ON MY CREATION AND NO REPLY TO YESTERDAY'S TELEXES AWAITING. VISITED SITE THIS MORNING (TUESDAY) FULLY EXPECTING TO FIND WORK IN PROGRESS. ASTOUNDED TO DISCOVER NO SIGN OF ACTIVITY.

GOD

TUESDAY
11.45 A.M.

AM STILL AWAITING YOUR REPLY. THIS REALLY IS BEYOND THE PALE.

WOULD POINT OUT THAT TODAY YOU ARE DUE TO DIVIDE WATERS THAT ARE UNDER FIRMAMENT, IN ADDITION TO DIVISION OF LIGHT FROM DARKNESS WHICH YOU NEGLECTED YESTERDAY.

WOULD DRAW YOUR ATTENTION TO PENALTY CLAUSE IN CONTRACT.

GOD

112 GOD G
123498 CONU G

God

Ted Slagworthy phoned while you were out at lunch. Very apologetic – said not to ge in a flap – would finish work sweat by Friday evening at late Sorry for delay – has had to fi off one or two outstanding jobs...
(then the pips went)

Veronica

ATTN: TED SLAGWORTHY

TUESDAY
2.30 P.M.

HAVE BEEN HANDED YOUR PHONE MESSAGE WHICH CAME THROUGH WHILE I WAS AT LUNCH. TRIED TO PHONE BACK BUT EACH TIME GOT A BUSY SIGNAL. ASSUME YOU HAVE TAKEN IT OFF HOOK.

FRANKLY NOT CONVINCED YOU WILL GET WORK DONE ON TIME. AND AM AS STONED = SORRY, ASTOUNDED = THAT YOU SHOULD TAKE ON OTHER WORK AT SUCH AN IMPORTANT TIME.

HAVE ACCORDINGLY INSTRUCTED MY BANKERS TO STOP ALL FURTHER PAYMENTS TO YOUR ACCOUNT UNTIL SATISFACTORY PROGRESS IS ESTABLISHED.

CONTACT ME AGAIN IMMEDIATELY OR CONSIDER YOURSELF IN BREACH OF CONTRACT.

GOD

G.

Mr. Slagworthy
phoned (again).
Seemed rather cross - muttered something
awfully rude - asked him to repeat it
but wouldn't.
Seemed very upset about "the readies"
(money?)
Said they would start work late this
afternoon and would have job finished
as promised.
Said something about keeping a "Bee
in your Bonnet" (?)
Asked if he'd like to speak to you
personally — rang off.
Veronica

ATTN: TED SLAGWORTHY

TUESDAY
3.45 P.M.

HAVE RECEIVED YOUR LATEST TELEPHONE MESSAGE. EXPECTED TO SPEAK PERSONALLY BUT MY SECRETARY SAYS YOU SEEMED BUSY AND DID NOT HAVE TIME TO WAIT.
DOUBT THIS VERY MUCH AND ASSUME IT WAS MERELY RELUCTANCE TO FACE UP TO YOUR RESPONSIBILITIES. I NOTE THAT YOU NOW INTEND TO START WORK LATE THIS AFTERNOON AND CONTINUE SOLIDLY FOR REST OF WEEK.
AFRAID I DO NOT SHARE YOUR OPTIMISM AND WILL CONTINUE TO SUSPEND PAYMENTS UNTIL AM ASSURED YOU CAN STILL COMPLETE ALL WORK IN WHAT IS NOW FOUR AND A QUARTER DAYS.

EXPECTING TO HEAR FROM YOU SHORTLY.

GOD

ATTN: GOD

TUESDAY
4.30 P.M.

HAVE STARTED WORK. DIVIDED LIGHT FROM DARKNESS AND DIVIDED WATERS UNDER FIRMAMENT. HAVE ALSO GATHERED TOGETHER THE WATERS UNDER THE HEAVEN UNTO ONE PLACE AND MADE A START ON BRINGING FORTH GRASS, THE HERB YIELDING SEED AND THE FRUIT TREE YIELDING FRUIT AFTER HIS KIND.

TRUST THIS NOW ALLOWS YOU TO INSTRUCT YOUR BANKER TO REINSTATE PAYMENTS.

REGARDS

TED SLAGWORTHY
UNIVERSAL CONSTRUCTION CO

TUESDAY
4.45 P.M.

HAVE RECEIVED YOUR TELEX WHICH QUITE FRANKLY STAGGERS ME. YOUR CLAIM TO HAVE COMPLETED VIRTUALLY THE FIRST THREE DAYS' CREATION IN LITTLE UNDER AN HOUR IS ONE I CANNOT ENTERTAIN. AT THAT RATE YOU WOULD BE ABLE TO COMPLETE THE WHOLE WORLD IN JUST TWO HOURS.

WILL VISIT SITE THIS EVENING (TUESDAY) TO INSPECT FOR MYSELF. UNTIL THEN WILL CONTINUE TO WITHHOLD PAYMENTS.

GOD

123498 CONU G
112 GOD G

ATTN: T. SLAGWORTHY

WEDNESDAY
9.45 A.M.

TOOK THE LIBERTY OF VISITING SITE LAST NIGHT (TUESDAY) TO CHECK ON YOUR CLAIMS AND IT WAS AS I HAD SUSPECTED. VIRTUALLY NONE OF THE WORK YOU CLAIMED FOR HAS BEEN DONE. I FOUND ONLY A LITTLE PATCH OF LIGHT THAT YOU APPEARED TO HAVE DIVIDED FROM THE DARKNESS AND A FEW HERBS.
OF COURSE, AS THERE WAS NO LIGHT IT WAS DIFFICULT TO INSPECT MUCH ELSE BUT I CERTAINLY COULDN'T SEE ANY DIVIDED WATERS, NOR WERE WATERS GATHERED TOGETHER.
MY SECRETARY HAS BEEN DISPATCHED TO REPORT. WIL…
CONTACT FURTHER WHEN HER FINDINGS ARE KNOWN.

GOD

112 GOD G
123498 CONU G

Progress — Wednesda…

1. ~~Ab~~ very little Lightness
2. Waters not gathered.
3. Only three herbs spotted.
4. Gardener installing herbs (a ~~sex~~ maniac)
5. Smell of gas.
6. Damp patches on firmament.
7. Electricity not working.
8. Litter everywhere
9. Portaloo on site not working
10. No grass!

11. No trees
12. No creatures that creepeth!
13. Mountains wrong size!!

123498 CONU G
112 GOD G

WEDNESDAY
12.15 P.M.

HAVE NOW SPOKEN TO MY SECRETARY WHO VISITED SITE AND APPEARS TO BE IN MUCH DISTRESS. NOT ONLY DID SHE HAVE TO WADE ABOUT KNEE-DEEP IN WATER IN SEMI-DARKNESS BUT THE PERSON YOU EMPLOYED TO BRING FORTH GRASS AND HERB YIELDING SEED AFTER HIS KIND VERY NEARLY MOLESTED HER AND SHE HAD TO LEAVE HURRIEDLY.

FROM WHAT LITTLE OF THE POOR GIRL'S ACCOUNT I COULD FOLLOW BETWEEN HER SOBS IT SEEMS YOUR CLAIMS WERE AS FANCIFUL AS I HAD FEARED.

AM THEREFORE CONTINUING TO WITHHOLD ALL PAYMENTS AND AM ALSO GETTING LEGAL ADVICE.

GOD

112 GOD G
123498 CONU G

123498 CONU G
112 GOD G

ATTN: TED SLAGWORTHY

WEDNESDAY
3.35 P.M

MY SECRETARY HAVING GONE OFF EARLY TO RECOVER I HAVE BEEN COMPELLED TO LOOK AFTER OFFICE. YOU CAN IMAGINE MY SHOCK WHEN I INADVERTENTLY SWITCHED ON THE TELEPHONE ANSWERING MACHINE AND HEARD YOUR VOICE. RARELY HAVE I HEARD SUCH LANGUAGE. I WOULD MOST CERTAINLY HAND OVER CONTENTS TO POLICE FOR INVESTIGATION WERE I LESS CHARITABLE. THINK YOURSELF LUCKY I AM.

MAY I PERHAPS PUT YOU RIGHT ON A FEW FACTS THAT YOUR STREAM OF ABUSE SEEMED TO NEGLECT.
FIRSTLY, YOU CONTRACTED TO SUPPLY ME WITH A WORLD OF SPECIFIED DESIGN WITHIN SIX DAYS. SECONDLY, YOU AGREED TO FOLLOW A MUTUALLY CONVENIENT PROGRESS CHART AND TO NOTIFY THIS OFFICE IF FOR ANY REASON YOU WERE UNABLE TO MEET SPECIFIED DATES. YOU HAVE CLEARLY FAILED ON BOTH POINTS. AND NO AMOUNT OF SLANDEROUS ILL-MOUTHED BAR-ROOM FILTH WILL PUT MATTERS STRAIGHT.

I AWAIT YOUR IMMEDIATE APOLOGY.

GOD

112 GOD G
123498 CONU G

112 GOD G
123498 CONU G

ATTN: GOD

THURSDAY
9.30 A.M.

SORRY ABOUT OUTBURST YESTERDAY. WAS QUITE WRONG OF
ME, AND IT WON'T HAPPEN AGAIN.

AM UNDER ENORMOUS PRESSURE OF LATE, AND NOT JUST FROM
CREATION OF YOUR WORLD. WOULD ORDINARILY HAVE HAD YOUR
WORLD STITCHED UP BY NOW, BUT SEEMS TO HAVE COME AT A
DIFFICULT TIME. IN ADDITION, AND I KNOW THIS ISN'T
REALLY ANY OF YOUR BUSINESS, MY WIFE HAS RECENTLY LEFT
ME FOR ANOTHER MAN, AND I HAVE BEEN FORCED TO LOOK AFTER
MY FOUR SMALL CHILDREN, ALL OF WHOM ARE UNDER FIVE AND
REQUIRE CONSTANT ATTENTION. ESPECIALLY THE SMALLEST WHO
IS JUST RECOVERING FROM A NEAR-FATAL ACCIDENT.

BUT YOU DON'T WANT TO HEAR OF MY PROBLEMS. WHY SHOULD
YOU CARE,JUST BECAUSE MY WIFE HAS THROWN A LIFETIME'S
DEVOTED LOVE BACK IN MY FACE AND LEFT ME A BROKEN MAN.

SORRY. I WAS GETTING CARRIED AWAY.

REST ASSURED WE'RE DOING OUR BEST UNDER DIFFICULT
CIRCUMSTANCES TO COMPLETE WORK ON TIME.

REGARDS

TED SLAGWORTHY

123498 CONU G
112 GOD G

"God"

Dear Mr. Slagworthy:

Re: Creation of The World

Thank you for your long and touching telex. While offering you any amount of compassion and sympathy, I'm afraid no amount of heart-rending misfortune can prevent me from commenting upon the abysmal scene which I encountered this morning (Thursday).

I visited the site then on my way to the office, and was optimistically entertaining the fanciful notion that I might see someone working. I was not expecting to see everyone and everything floating in 10 feet of deep thick slime. Some other pertinent points which I noted were:

1. Land in the wrong place
2. No hills
3. Only one fish
4. Gross irregularities in employees' pension and insurance contributions.

In addition, the mountains (both of them) had been installed upside-down; all three rivers ran uphill; and what remained of the insects appeared to have been assembled with nuts and bolts.

Yours,

Veronica Makepiece

for GOD

G:VM

DICTATED BUT NOT READ

P.S. Re: the agreed schedule (Section 7 (B)/1 paragraph 8, line 31. For "Russian Urinals to be 2,000 miles long," substitute "Russian Urals to be 2,000 miles long."

112 GOD G

ATTN: GOD

THURSDAY

12.30 P.M.

ARRIVED AT SITE AT 11.15 TO FIND WORKMEN TAKING A BREAK. SAID THEY HAD JUST THAT MINUTE STOPPED WORK. COULD SEE NO SIGN OF ACTIVITY. ASKED VARIOUS SEARCHING QUESTIONS, BUT THEY PRETENDED TO BE FOREIGN AND SAID 'QUE?' A LOT.

EVERYONE HAS GONE TO LUNCH NOW. WILL REPORT AGAIN THIS AFTERNOON.

VERONICA

112 GOD G

ATTN: GOD

THURSDAY

3.35 P.M.

RETURNED TO SITE AT 2.30 TO FIND NO ONE BACK FROM LUNCH. RETURNED AT 3.00. STRONG SMELL OF BEER, AND WORKMEN HAVING ANOTHER BREAK. SAID 'HOW CURIOUS YOU ALWAYS SEEM TO COME JUST AFTER WE'VE DONE A PARTICULARLY STRENUOUS BIT OF WORK.' ASKED THEM MORE SEARCHING QUESTIONS BUT THEY JUST PICKED UP AND WENT HOME.

VERONICA

123498 CONU G
112 GOD G

ATTN: TED SLAGWORTHY

THURSDAY
3.50 P.M.

APPALLING REPORTS ABOUT THE SITE FROM MY SECRETARY.
DEMAND YOU TAKE SITUATION IN HAND OR ALL HELL WILL
BE LET LOOSE.

GOD

112 GOD G
123498 CONU G

ATTN: GOD

THURSDAY
4.20 P.M.

SORRY TO HEAR YOU'RE NOT HAPPY. SUGGEST YOU DON'T WORRY.
SUGGEST YOU KEEP AL HELL CHAINED UP. SUGGEST YOU
INSTRUCT YOUR BANKERS TO REINSTATE PAYMENTS. SUGGEST
YOU TAKE A NICE LONG HOLIDAY AS IT'S OBVIOUSLY ALL
GETTING TOO MUCH FOR YOU.

KIND REGARDS.

TED

123498 CONU G
112 GOD G

ATTN: T.G. COHEN

FRIDAY
9.15 A.M.

WORLD COMING ON PRETTY WELL. SLIGHT DELAY OVER ONE OR TWO ITEMS BUT OTHERWISE NO PROBLEMS. JUST WHAT WE ALL HAD IN MIND. E[illegible]NG LOOKING REALLY GOOD AND THINK YOU WILL BE IM[illegible]

GOD

ATTN: T. SLAGWORTHY

FRIDAY
10.23 A.M.

WHAT THE DEVIL IS GOING ON? MY SECRETARY HAS JUST RETURNED FROM SITE IN STATE OF SHOCK. SAYS THE WHOLE SHAMBLES IS LOOKING WORSE THAN EVER! NOTHING COMPLETE! LAZY WORKMEN! LAND STILL IN WRONG PLACE! INSECTS ALL FLOWN AWAY! HERBS HAVE LEAF MOLD!

TELEX YOUR IMMEDIATE REPLY.

GOD

ATTN: T.G. COHEN

FRIDAY
12.05 P.M.

THANKS FOR LATEST LETTER. NOTE YOU ARE PLANNING TO POP OVER TO SITE, BUT SUGGEST IT MIGHT PERHAPS BE BETTER NOT TO RIGHT NOW. MIGHT UPSET BUILDERS. THESE CREATIVE CHAPS CAN BE TEMPERAMENTAL.

HOW ABOUT TOMORROW AFTERNOON INSTEAD?

(NOTHING TO WORRY ABOUT ... WORLD LOOKING REALLY FANTASTIC.)

KIND REGARDS

GOD

ATTN: T. SLAGWORTHY

FRIDAY
12.10 P.M.

STILL NOT HEARD A THING FROM YOU AND, TO MAKE MATTERS WORSE, COSMIC FINANCIAL ARE NOW ON MY BACK.

ATTN: T.G. COHEN

FRIDAY
2.05 P.M.

HAVE JUST RECEIVED YOUR TELEPHONE MESSAGE.
REGRET I AM UNABLE TO MEET YOU OVER AT THE WORLD
THIS EVENING. THERE'S A VERY, VERY THICK FOG
THERE AT MOMENT (BUILDERS TRYING OUT NEW FOG MACHINE.)
AND IT WILL BE DARK SOON, SO YOU WON'T SEE ANYTHING
ANYWAY.

SUGGEST WE GO TOMORROW OR THEREABOUTS. BETTER TO
WAIT UNTIL ALL WORK ABSOLUTELY COMPLETE SO YOU CAN
REALLY GET FEEL OF PLACE. WILL CONTACT TOMORROW
TO FIX CONVENIENT TIME.

KIND REGARDS.

GOD

123498 CONU G
112 GOD

ATTN: SLAGWORTHY

FRIDAY
2.55 P.M.

REPLY OR ELSE.

GOD

ATTN: TED SLAGWORTHY

FRIDAY
3.32 P.M.

RECEIVED YOUR PHONE MESSAGE. NO! WON'T WAIT TILL MONDAY!
IMPERATIVE THAT CREATION OF WHOLE WORLD BE COMPLETE BY
TOMORROW EVENING.

INCIDENTALLY, DON'T BELIEVE FOR A MOMENT THAT YOUR POOR
OLD MOTHER IS CALLING FOR YOU FROM HOSPITAL BED. IN
FACT, DON'T BELIEVE A SINGLE WORD YOU SAY. SKIP THE
EXCUSES.

COMPLETE BY TOMORROW!

GOD

234987 AMALWORLD
112 GOD G
0001/AB

ATTN: T.G. C

FRIDAY
4.40 P.M.

SO GLAD TO HEAR YOU'VE DECIDED NOT TO VISIT WORLD
THIS EVENING AFTER ALL. AM SURE DECISION IS FOR
THE BEST.

GOD

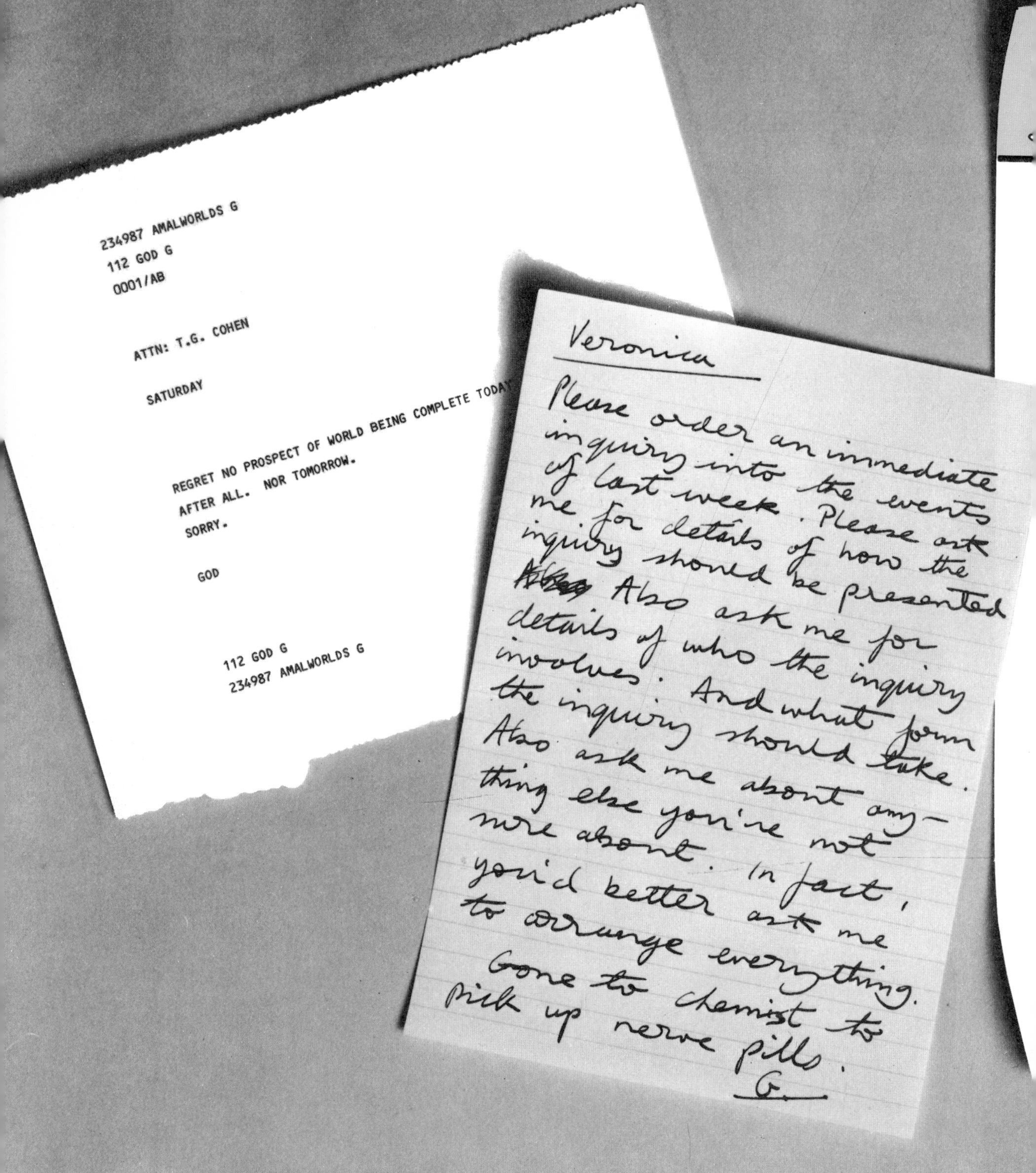

234987 AMALWORLDS G
112 GOD G
0001/AB

ATTN: T.G. COHEN

SATURDAY

REGRET NO PROSPECT OF WORLD BEING COMPLETE TODAY
AFTER ALL. NOR TOMORROW.
SORRY.

GOD

112 GOD G
234987 AMALWORLDS G

Veronica

Please order an immediate inquiry into the events of last week. Please ask me for details of how the inquiry should be presented. ~~Also~~ Also ask me for details of who the inquiry involves. And what form the inquiry should take. Also ask me about anything else you're not sure about. In fact, you'd better ask me to arrange everything.

Gone to chemist to pick up nerve pills.

G.

"God"

ar Mr. Slagworthy:

Re: Creation of The World

I cannot trust myself to write this
tter sanely, so great is my anger!

Last week an utterly horrendous
ries of events took place as a result
the work carried out (or not) in
e name of your company. I hold you
rsonally responsible. I have ordered
formal inquiry into the full details,
t from my limited inquiries it would
pear you took the very least possible
re and effort in all aspects of the
rk.

I now have to face the embarrassing
d thoroughly unappetizing prospect of
grilling from Cosmic Financial
rporation, for which I am sure to
y heavily. This creation was
pposed to be an unforgettable event;
event that would be written about
d talked of for centuries. Instead,
has proved to be totally forgettable
inly because nothing actually
ppened to remember it by.

I shall be writing to you in more
tail later but, meanwhile, I expec
see you in my office tomorrow
uesday) morning without fail to a
l my questions in this matter.

Yours frothingly,

Veronica Makepiece

For GOD

VM

CTATED BUT NOT READ

G.

Mr. Cohen phoned while
you were at the psychoanalyst's.
V. difficult to hear what he said –
earpiece too hot to put near ear.
Not v. coherent, either!
Seemed V. V. angry.
Said you were to call him the minute
you put so much as a toe through
the door. Said something else about
fingernails being torn out. Also
gave a fairly graphic description
of what happened to people who let
him down (attached. Sorry – pen ran
out after 16 pages).
Think you should phone him. Don't
think I can stand much more!

Veronica

Phone Message: God.

Man from the Hillock Department of Mountain Supply shop rang while you were at the clinic having your face lift. Said he'd got 6 small mountains we'd ordered from him five months ago and could we come round and collect them as they were blocking the ware-house.

Veronica

Telephone Message

TIME RECEIVED ____ DATE ____

FROM ____

GOD

MR. (SOUNDED LIKE 'R. MEBLOODY-LEGG) PHONED. SOUNDED VERY AGITATED. SAID WE ORDERED 75,000 'BEASTS THAT MOVETH' FROM HIM SOME WHILE AGO AND DID WE STILL WANT THEM? SAID THEY WERE CLUTTERING UP HIS WAREHOUSE AND MAKING HIS LIFE HELL (ALSO MAKING HIS LIFE DANGEROUS). ASKED IF WE COULD PHONE HIM BACK - BUT BEFORE HE COULD REPLY THERE WAS A ~~STRANGE~~ STRANGE SORT OF THROTTLED SCREAM AND THE LINE WENT DEAD. VERONICA

RECEIVED BY ____

"God"

Dear God:

It is with regret that we, the under-signed, write to inform you that we wish to tender our resignation to take effect as from today.

We regret that we can no longer tolerate the work or the atmosphere in the office and wish to leave before it is too late. This was once a happy staff and pleasant work. However, the work and effort put into the creation of the World has turned this place into a madhouse and we do not feel able to remain here a moment longer.

Regretfully yours,

Janice
Winston
Vince
Harriet

Keith
Tony
Eamonn
Gary

John
Mark
Luke
Matthew

Norman
Denise
Elvis
The office cat

DEAR GOD,
WEATHER FINE! FOOD GREAT! WILD NIGHTLIFE! WISH YOU WERE HERE.
HAVE DECIDED TO SPEND ~~A FEW DAYS~~ ~~A WEEK~~ A FORTNIGHT OR SO HERE AT THE SEASIDE.

P.S. FORGOT TO SWITCH OFF WATER WHEN WE LEFT. PSE DO US V. BIG FAVOUR - NIP OVER THERE AND SWITCH IT OFF. STOPCOCK IS SOMEWHERE UNDER NORTH AFRICA.

UNIVERSAL

POSTCARD

AFFIX STAMP HERE

NAME GOD

ADDRESS UNIT 4
LEVEL 2
CENTRAL PLAZA.

The view shows the attractive Solarium and Massage Parlour shortly before a raid by Vice Squad detectives.

0001/AB

ATTN: GOD

MOST, MOST URGENT WHAT IN THE WORLD IS GOING ON EXPECTED ALL WORK TO BE COMPLETED BY NOW. MOST ANXIOUS THAT THIS BE DONE BY NINE O'CLOCK MONDAY MORNING WITHOUT FAIL OR I'LL BE ROUND TO GIVE YOU WHAT-FOR PERSONALLY.

MOST = REPEAT MOST = URGENT

T.G. Cohen

T.G. COHEN

"God"

Dear Mr. Slagworthy:

Re: The Creation Of The World

Thank you for your letter and invoice, both of which I have thrown straight into the waste basket. I am quite unable to recall another occasion on which I have been so angry though, goodness knows, during the course of this project there have been plenty of opportunities.

Not only do I consider your request for payment an impudent act of bravado following your appalling record to date, but I also consider the request for the full amount quite outrageous in view of the fact that you have barely completed the first quarter of the work required.

You may be certain that your invoice will not be paid in 30 days as you request. Nor in 60 days. Nor in 180 days. In fact, I doubt that if you lived to be 150 you would see it paid! I suggest that if you want so much as to smell even a penny of the settlement you will (a) show that you are willing to complete the work in hand diligently, responsibly and thoroughly; and (b) convey such an intention at the earliest opportunity.

Until such time, I do not wish to see or hear from your company again.

Yours disgustedly,

Veronica Makepiece

for GOD

G:VM

DICTATED BUT NOT READ

Telephone Message

TIME RECEIVED 10 45 DATE

FROM Mr. SLAGWORTHY

GOD

MR. SLAGWORTHY PHONED. SAID 'HOW ABOUT TUESDAY?' – TOLD HIM I WAS BUSY. HE SAID 'NO, HOW ABOUT TUESDAY FOR THE MEETING?' SAID WE WOULD CONFIRM.

RECEIVED BY Veronica

"God"

Dear Mr. Slagworthy,

Re: Creation Of The World

I look forward to seeing you at 9.00 very, very sharp in my office on Tuesday morning.

Be punctual.

Yours briefly,

Tanya Starr

for God

Minutes of Meeting Held 9.00 a.m. Tuesday to Discuss

THE CREATION OF THE WORLD

Those present: God

Mr. Slagworthy (Universal Construction Co.)

The following points were raised:

1. God called Mr. Slagworthy a [redacted] !
2. God also called Mr. Slagworthy a [redacted] [redacted] !
3. God intimated that Mr. Slagworthy could [redacted] [redacted] [redacted] !
4. God paused for breath
5. Mr. Slagworthy apologised
6. God said apologies weren't enough
7. Mr. Slagworthy grovelled on his knees and apologised profusely
8. God said all right, all right he accepted the apologies
9. Mr. Slagworthy said good, how about some money?
10. God called Mr. Slagworthy an [redacted] [redacted] [redacted] !
11. Mr. Slagworthy said thank you
12. God said when could work be expected to start again?
13. Mr. Slagworthy said he must be leaving
14. God said when could work be expected to start again?
15. Mr. Slagworthy put on his hat and coat
16. God tied Mr. Slagworthy to a chair with a piece of string
17. God said now, when could work be expected to start again?
18. Mr. Slagworthy said stop, stop, you're hurting me
19. Mr. Slagworthy said two weeks on Friday
20. Mr. Slagworthy said stop, stop, I can't breathe
21. Mr. Slagworthy said next Thursday
22. God said this was hurting him more than it was hurting Mr. Slagworthy

Mr. Slagworthy said tomorrow

God tightened the thumbscrews

Mr. Slagworthy promised tomorrow and said he'd put it in writing

God passed him a pen and a piece of paper

Mr. Slagworthy said he didn't know how to write

God taught him

Mr. Slagworthy mentioned the word reluctance a lot

God mentioned the word violence a lot

God and Mr. Slagworthy shook hands

MEETING CLOSED

234987 AMALWORLDS G

112 GOD G

ATTN: T.G. COHEN

VERY CORDIAL MEETING TODAY BETWEEN SELF AND BUILDER. AMICABLY AGREED THAT WORK ON CREATION WOULD START TOMORROW (WEDNESDAY) AND BE FINISHED WITHIN FIVE DAYS WITHOUT FAIL.

GOD

234987 AMALWORLDS G

112 GOD G

0001/AB

ATTN: T.G. COHEN

HAVE INSTALLED PERMANENT OVERSEER AT SITE TO REPORT ON PROGRESS. BUILDERS HAVE STARTED TO CLEAR SITE. HAVE ALSO MANAGED TO INSTALL LIMITED SOURCE OF LIGHT AND DARKNESS. FIRST TESTS OF EVERY THING THAT CREEPETH DUE TO START THIS AFTERNOON. HERB YIELDING SEED NOW PLANTED AND PROVING SUCCESSFUL.

SLIGHT PROBLEM WITH GREAT WHALES BUT HAVE ORDERED HALF-A-DOZEN MORE. ALSO ICE CAPS KEEP SLIPPING AND HAVE HAD TO BE SCREWED DOWN IN PLACE FOR TIME BEING.

REGARDS.

GOD

Telephone Message

TIME RECEIVED 12·30 DATE

FROM OVERSEER

OVERSEER PHONED WHILE YOU WERE OUT AT THE COBBLER'S. REPORTS PROGRESS STIL GOING REASONABLY WELL, BUT SLIGHT PROBLEM WITH FISH. GILLS APPARENTLY FAULTY. SO FAR 20,000 DEAD, BUT HAVE MANAGED TO HIDE THEM ALL UNDER BELGIUM. SLIGHT SMELL, BUT THINKS IT WILL DIE AWAY.

RECEIVED BY VERONICA

Telephone Message

TIME RECEIVED 2·30 DATE

FROM - OVERSEER

GOD

OVERSEER PHONED TO REPORT PROGRESS GOING 'REASONABLY'. LIGHT AND DARKNESS NOW SPLIT. HINGES PUT ON ITALY. NEW OASTLINES FITTED TO SWITZERLAND. STILL ROBLEM WITH BELGIUM (BEGINNING TO IELL QUITE CONSIDERABLY)

CEIVED BY VERONICA

Telephone Message

TIME RECEIVED 3.40 DATE

FROM OVERSEER

OVERSEER CALLED TO SAY WORK 'STILL PROGRESSING'. LIGHT AND DARKNESS FAILED (TWICE). BELGIUM SMELLING ABOMINABLY AND HAS TO BE TOWED INTO MIDDLE OF ATLANTIC OCEAN. ICELAND FITTED WRONG WAY ROUND BUT TOO LATE TO DO ANYTHING ABOUT IT.

RECEIVED BY VERONICA.

IVED 4·20 DATE

FROM OVERSEER

HAVING PROBLEMS WITH NORTH AMERICA. WON'T FIT. MIGHT HAVE TO SAW OFF IRELAND AND PUT IT SOMEWHERE ELSE. NORWAY HAS GOT SOME RATHER NASTY SCORCH MARKS AS A RESULT OF A FIRE. WILL REPORT AGAIN TOMORROW.

RECEIVED BY VERONICA.

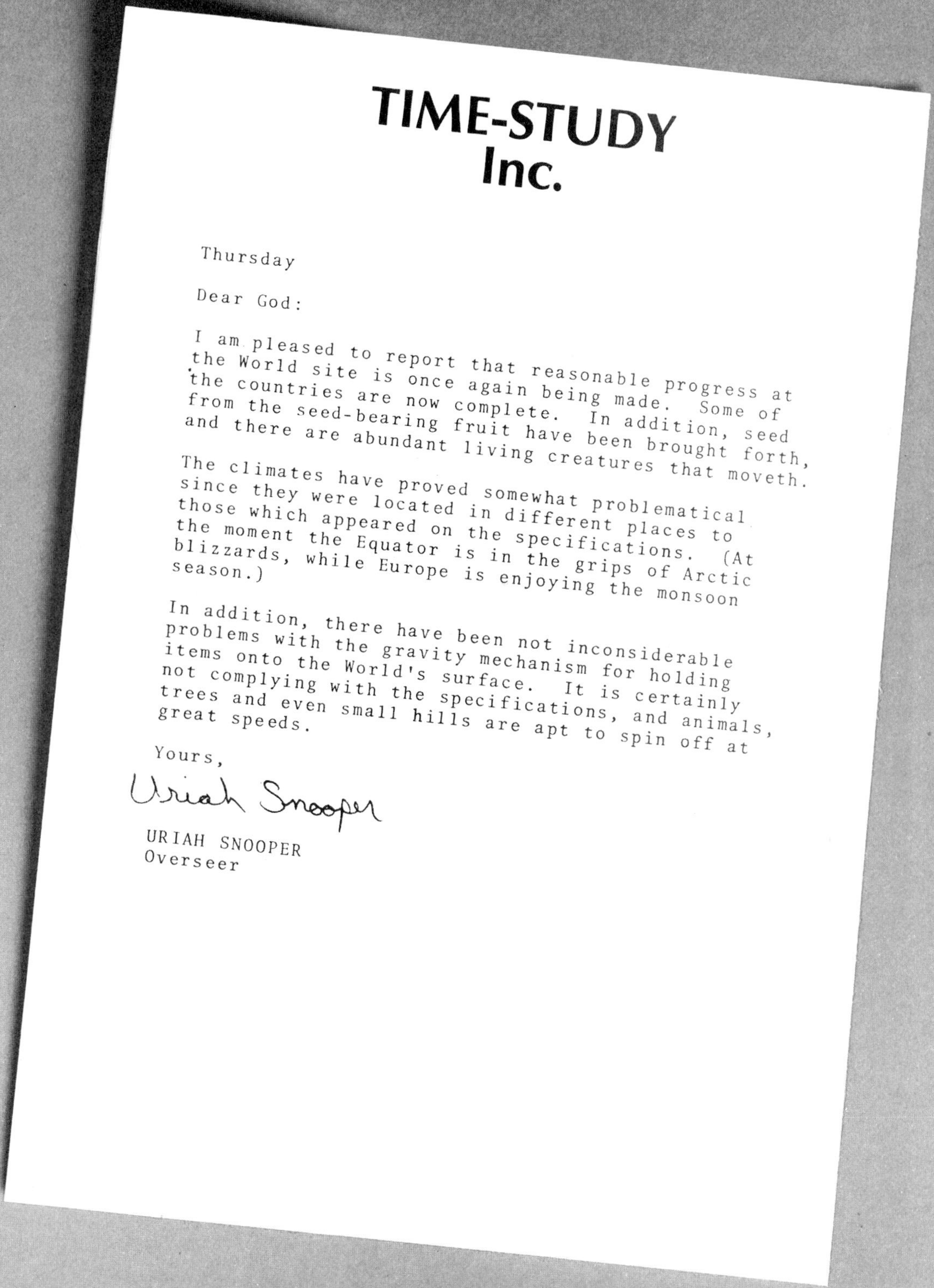

TIME-STUDY Inc.

Thursday

Dear God:

I am pleased to report that reasonable progress at the World site is once again being made. Some of the countries are now complete. In addition, seed from the seed-bearing fruit have been brought forth, and there are abundant living creatures that moveth.

The climates have proved somewhat problematical since they were located in different places to those which appeared on the specifications. (At the moment the Equator is in the grips of Arctic blizzards, while Europe is enjoying the monsoon season.)

In addition, there have been not inconsiderable problems with the gravity mechanism for holding items onto the World's surface. It is certainly not complying with the specifications, and animals, trees and even small hills are apt to spin off at great speeds.

Yours,

Uriah Snooper

URIAH SNOOPER
Overseer

"God"

Friday

Dear Mr. Cohen:

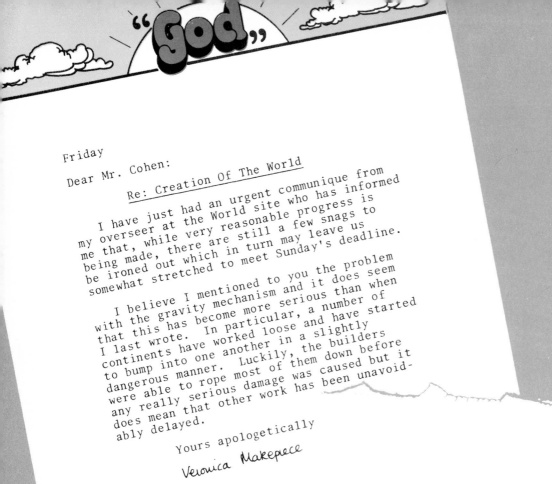

Re: Creation Of The World

I have just had an urgent communique from my overseer at the World site who has informed me that, while very reasonable progress is being made, there are still a few snags to be ironed out which in turn may leave us somewhat stretched to meet Sunday's deadline.

I believe I mentioned to you the problem with the gravity mechanism and it does seem that this has become more serious than when I last wrote. In particular, a number of continents have worked loose and have started to bump into one another in a slightly dangerous manner. Luckily, the builders were able to rope most of them down before any really serious damage was caused but it does mean that other work has been unavoidably delayed.

Yours apologetically

Veronica Makepeace

for GOD

G:VM

DICTATED BUT NOT READ

ATTN: GOD

IN RECEIPT OF YOUR LETTER. CONTENTS NOT AT ALL WELL RECEIVED HERE AT COSMIC FINANCIAL. PLS OBTAIN IMMEDIA A REALISTIC INDICATION AS TO WHEN WORLD LIKELY TO BE COMPLETED. TELEX DETAILS AT ONCE.

T.G. COHEN

"God"

CREATION OF THE WORLD

OFFICIAL transcripts of meeting between God and Universal Construction Co. to discuss further progress on the above project.

1. It was reported that the problems with the gravity mechanism were far more serious than at first anticipated and could not be resolved with the materials available.

2. It was suggested that if the world was to revolve at a much slower speed things might not fly off quite so readily. However, it was pointed out that if the world revolved at a slower speed it would be liable to upset the delicate light-darkness mechanism and lead to it being pitch black at lunchtime and bright and clear at midnight.

3. It was suggested that if continents could be nailed down the gravity problem might be overcome. However, it was also suggested that this solution could not be applied to the creeping things that creepeth, or to the fish that swimmeth, or the winged fowl that flyeth, all of whom would prove very difficult to nail down. However, it was agreed to sanction experiments to see if fish could not be nailed to the ground without causing undue stress or suffering. Mr. Slagworthy said he knew of a firm who specialized in just such work and would contact them to see if they would be willing to carry out the experiments.

4. It was also pointed out that several other problems had arisen that could not have been anticipated. It was reported that the artificial grass was not suitable for grazing animals since the beasts were showing a tendency to become very thin and die of starvation.

5. It was pointed out to the builders that the one bag of sand listed in the specifications was insufficient to cover the large amount of desert-land required, and it was agreed that Cosmic & Universal Construction should provide at no extra cost another half-dozen bags.

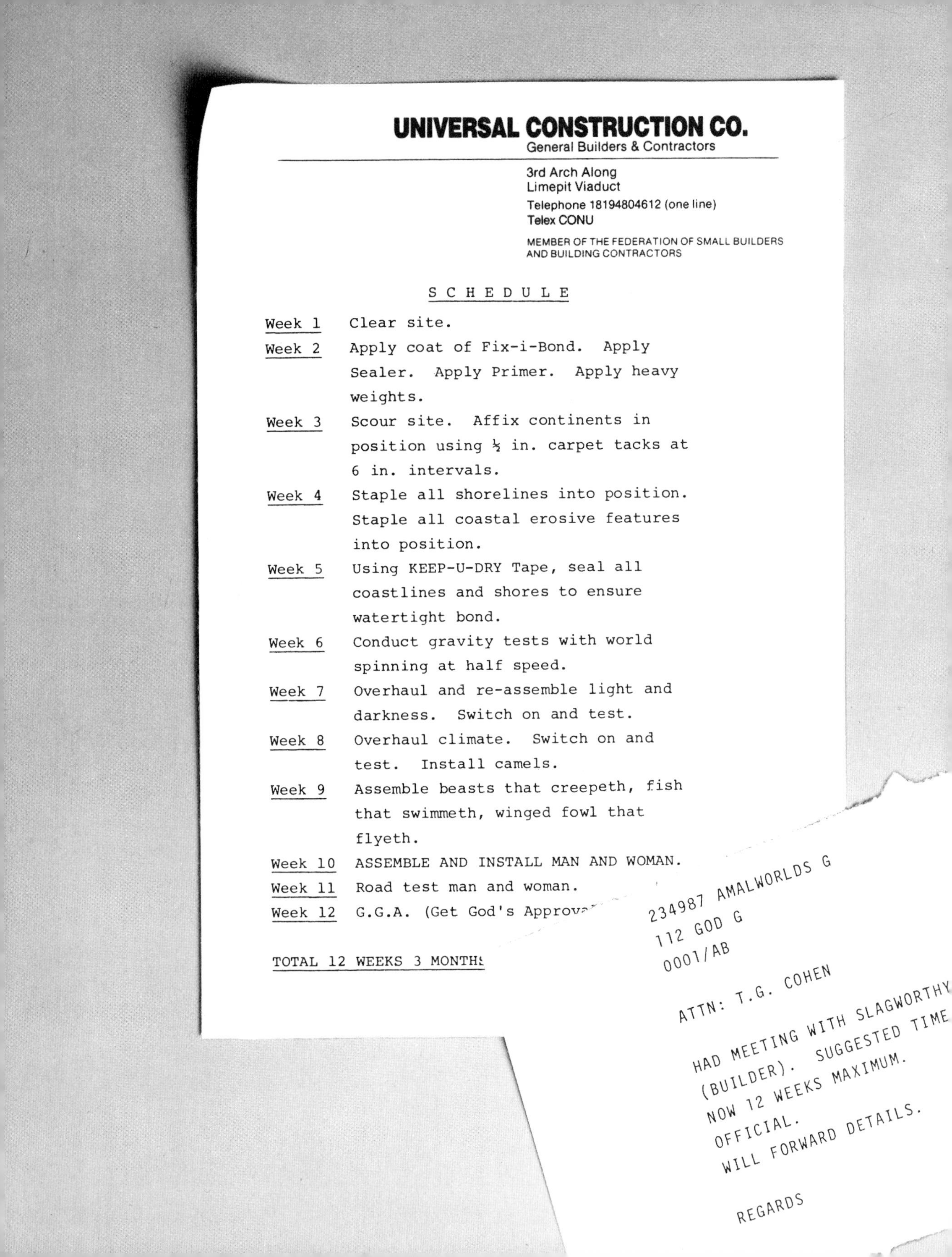

UNIVERSAL CONSTRUCTION CO.
General Builders & Contractors

3rd Arch Along
Limepit Viaduct
Telephone 18194804612 (one line)
Telex CONU

MEMBER OF THE FEDERATION OF SMALL BUILDERS AND BUILDING CONTRACTORS

S C H E D U L E

Week 1 Clear site.

Week 2 Apply coat of Fix-i-Bond. Apply Sealer. Apply Primer. Apply heavy weights.

Week 3 Scour site. Affix continents in position using ½ in. carpet tacks at 6 in. intervals.

Week 4 Staple all shorelines into position. Staple all coastal erosive features into position.

Week 5 Using KEEP-U-DRY Tape, seal all coastlines and shores to ensure watertight bond.

Week 6 Conduct gravity tests with world spinning at half speed.

Week 7 Overhaul and re-assemble light and darkness. Switch on and test.

Week 8 Overhaul climate. Switch on and test. Install camels.

Week 9 Assemble beasts that creepeth, fish that swimmeth, winged fowl that flyeth.

Week 10 ASSEMBLE AND INSTALL MAN AND WOMAN.

Week 11 Road test man and woman.

Week 12 G.G.A. (Get God's Approv

TOTAL 12 WEEKS 3 MONTH

234987 AMALWORLDS G
112 GOD G
0001/AB

ATTN: T.G. COHEN

HAD MEETING WITH SLAGWORTHY
(BUILDER). SUGGESTED TIME
NOW 12 WEEKS MAXIMUM.
OFFICIAL.
WILL FORWARD DETAILS.

REGARDS

123498 CONU G
112 GOD G

ATTN: GOD

HAVE BEGUN (AGAIN). TRIED TO SOLVE GRAVITY PROBLEMS. IMMEDIATE SNAG. WORLD WILL NOT REVOLVE NOW. MECHANISM SEIZED UP. TRIED TO FREE IT WITH MECHANICAL DIGGER. DIGGER RUINED. WORLD NOW TILTED TO ONE SIDE. NOW RESTING ON TWO BRICKS AND BLOCK OF WOOD.

PLEASE ADVISE.

TED SLAGWORTHY

123498 CONU G
112 GOD G

123498 CONU G
112 GOD G

ATTN: GOD

GOOD NEWS - WORLD NOW REVOLVING AGAIN. BAD NEWS - REVOLVING IN REVERSE. ALL VEGETATION RIPPED OFF. BIRDS FLYING BACKWARDS.

WIRING ON CLIMATES BURNT OUT. SNOW FALLING ALTHOUGH TEMPERATURE OVER 105°F. HEAT HAS CAUSED CONTINENTS TO COME UNSTUCK. FIX-I-BOND GLUE EVERYWHERE. ANIMALS STUCK TO CONTINENTS.

TED SLAGWORTHY
123498 CONU G
112 GOD G

God

Surveyor phoned to report on state of creation. Sounded V. distraught. Said he was a surveyor, not a magician! Said he was returning our fee as he was unable to complete the work under any circumstances. Asked if I should get you to contact him but he just started to cry and hung up.

Veronica

112 GOD G
234987 AMALWORLDS G
0001/AB

ATTN: GOD

WHAT IS HAPPENING? YOU'VE BEEN REMARKABLY QUIET OF LATE. REPORT AT ONCE. AM UNDER ENORMOUS PRESSURE FROM MANAGING DIRECTOR.

T.G. COHEN

234987 AMAL
112 GOD G

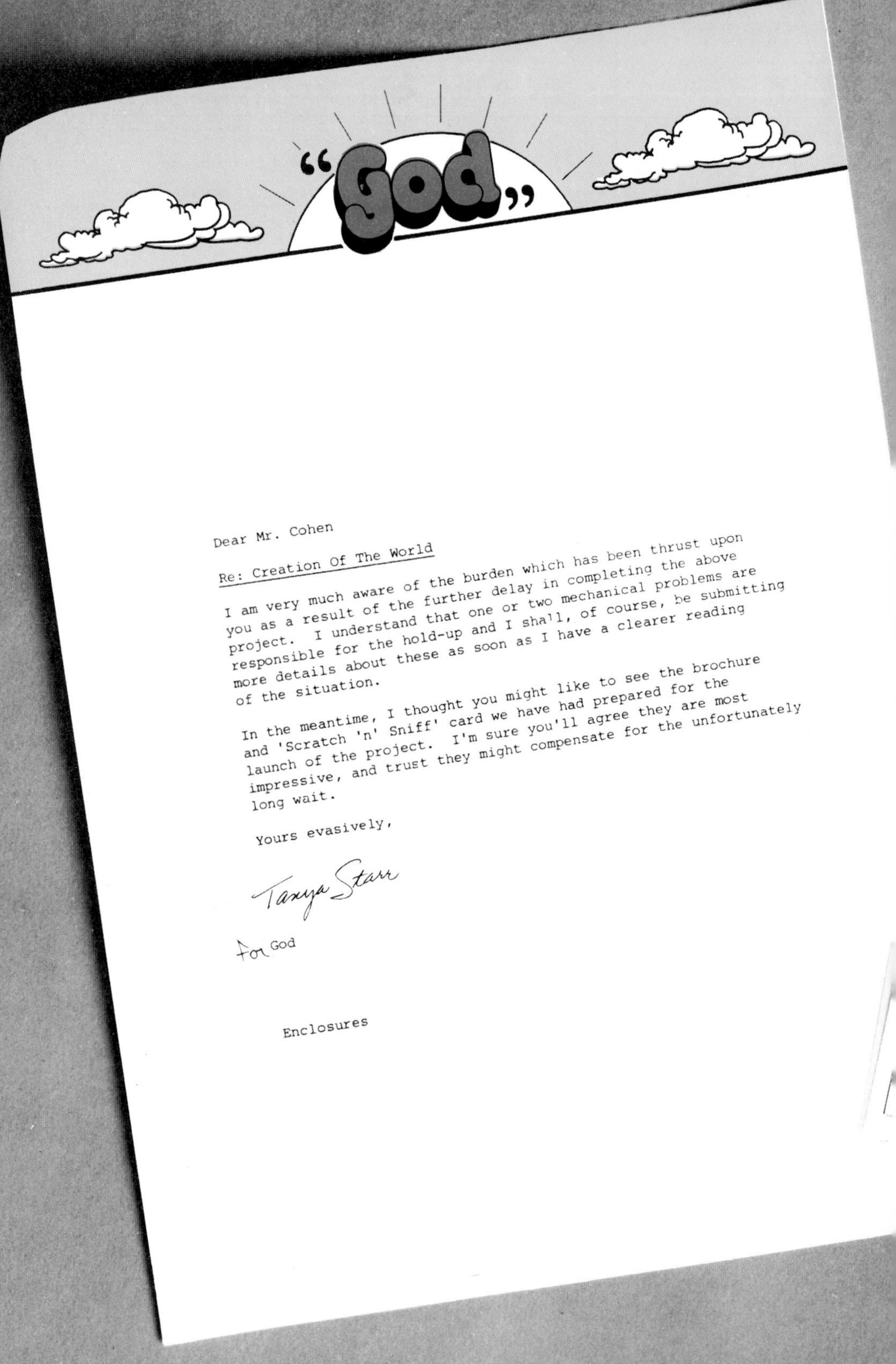

Dear Mr. Cohen

Re: Creation Of The World

I am very much aware of the burden which has been thrust upon you as a result of the further delay in completing the above project. I understand that one or two mechanical problems are responsible for the hold-up and I shall, of course, be submitting more details about these as soon as I have a clearer reading of the situation.

In the meantime, I thought you might like to see the brochure and 'Scratch 'n' Sniff' card we have had prepared for the launch of the project. I'm sure you'll agree they are most impressive, and trust they might compensate for the unfortunately long wait.

Yours evasively,

Tanya Starr

for God

Enclosures

A BRAND NEW WORLD!

A world created for you ... your children ... and your children's children. A world planned in meticulous detail because we believe that, if a world is worth creating at all, it's worth creating well. So you can be sure it will work – day in, day out. It's a world you will be proud of. A world you'll never want to leave. Because it's YOUR world.

Features include: 'Rock effect' on all mountain faces/intertropical convergence zone/edible wildlife/Salopian outwash fans/tight T-shirts/Malaysia/marshland scenery/geyers/fault line scarps/Bolton/transfluent laterite soils/squally showers/quicksand/proluval stratigraphy/Glasgow/tors/nubile 16-year old schoolgirls/truncated spurs/isothermic gradients/peek-a-boo bras/trade winds/Hull/barrier reefs/fenland/graded sediment/prairies/loam/France/ready-made fossils/firm young bosoms thrusting against see-through negligées/selva/tornadoes/Germany (x2)/monoliths/Cyprus/clinographic curves.

INCLUDES Thermal cladding; insulation; fail-safe device; dead man's handle; auxiliary brakes; automatic cut-out; electrical valves; self-lubricating axis; thermostatic control; ceramic chip-proof finish; posture springing; lumbar support.

SPECIAL CHARACTERISTICS
Man and Woman • Integral hills • Wet water • Non-combustible wildlife • Full range of climates • Diverse trees • Wide selection of plants • Unique smell • Automatic night and day • Choice of countries • Beasts that creepeth • Vegetation that doesn't creepeth all that much.

SPAIN!*
As a special bonus with this – and only this – world, we are supplying you with a free Spain for you to install and use however you see fit (machine gun and rifles not included).
** or cash equivalent.*

NO ARTIFICIAL INGREDIENTS
We have used no artificial ingredients in preparing this world. Not many, anyway. Well, certainly not all that many we're prepared to tell you about.

IT'S OUR WORLD
We have built this world large enough so there's space for everyone. Space to breathe. Space to spread. Space to do anything else you had in mind*. You'll never feel cramped, no matter how large your requirements. Which is why you'll never mind saying 'It's *Our* World'.
** see doctor for full details.*

OWN MAN AND WOMAN!!
The world comes complete with ready-made, fully assembled man and woman (batteries not included). Made to highest specifications imaginable. Each man and woman outfit includes spare ear, spare leg, spare teeth and spare femero-cutaneous nerve.

*Finger Not Included

OFFICIAL SCRATCH 'N' SNIFF CARD

Enjoy the smells of the new World
IN THE COMFORT OF YOUR OWN HOME!

Simply scratch* then sniff to enjoy the smell of:

Mountain	Tree	Gas	Boiled Cabbage	Sea
Man	Man's Armpit	Fish	Dead Fish	Wet Fish
Wet Clothes	Wet Paint	Foxgloves	Cloves	Chicken Droppings
Apple Blossom	Sour Milk	Camel's Breath	Sweaty Bodies	Antiseptic
Chanel No. 5	Chanel No. 6	Playboy Channel	Water	Roses
Cold Meat Sandwiches	Sewers	Fresh Air	Fresh Flowers	Popcorn
Germany	Belgium	Tulips	Warm Tracksuits	French Person

112 GOD G

ATTN: GOD

GLAD TO REPORT PROGRESS. SEAS NOW UNPACKED AND IN FULL WORKING ORDER. HOLLYHOCKS = SORRY, HILLOCKS = NOW INSTALLED AND LOOKING GOOD.

HOWEVER, SOMEONE LEFT MONSOON CLIMATE ON OVERNIGHT AND MUCH OF ASIA DAMAGED. HUNG ON LINE TO DRY. PLEASE CONFIRM WE CAN CLAIM ON INSURANCE.

ANTELOPE YOU SUPPLIED FAULTY ... KEEPS TRYING TO BREED WITH MONKEYS. TREES A BIT SMALL ... KEEP TRIPPING OVER THEM.

OTHERWISE OK.

TED SLAGWORTHY

123498 CONU G

112 GOD G

ATTN: GOD

NEVER MIND THE BROCHURE AND THAT SMELLY THING, HOW'S THE WORK PROGRESSING? DEMAND YOU GET IN TOUCH IMMEDIATELY TO ADVISE.

COHEN

112 GOD G

ATTN: GOD

REGRET TO REPORT NUMBER OF MISHAPS. DUE TO UNFORTUNATE TYPING ERROR ON ORDER FORM, HAVE JUST TAKEN DELIVERY OF BREASTS THAT CREEPETH.

NUMBER OF ELEPHANTS KILLED. SUGGEST WE REMOVE WINGS, OR AT LEAST CLIP THEM.

95 FEET OF SNOW IN COLORADO. IS THIS RIGHT (NOT ON SPECIFICATIONS)? SUGGEST YOU SUPPLY SHOVEL AND SNOWPLOUGH.

HOLDING YOU RESPONSIBLE FOR ACCIDENTS/FAULTS/ DELAYS. YOU OBVIOUSLY WOULDN'T RECOGNISE A COMPETENT SUPPLIER IF ONE CAME UP AND KICKED YOU ON THE SHIN.

TED SLAGWOR

123498 CONU G

112 GOD G

ATTN: GOD

OUR REPORTS SHOW INSPECTOR'S PROCEDURES OVERLOOKED/ INATTENTION TO DETAIL/INSUFFICIENT CARE AND CONTROL/ MISMANAGEMENT/MALADMINISTRATION.

ALSO, CHART SHOWS WORK FALLING BEHIND ON ALL SCHEDULES.

REPORT NOW.

T.G. COHEN

234987 AMALWORLDS G

"God"

Dear Mr. Cohen:

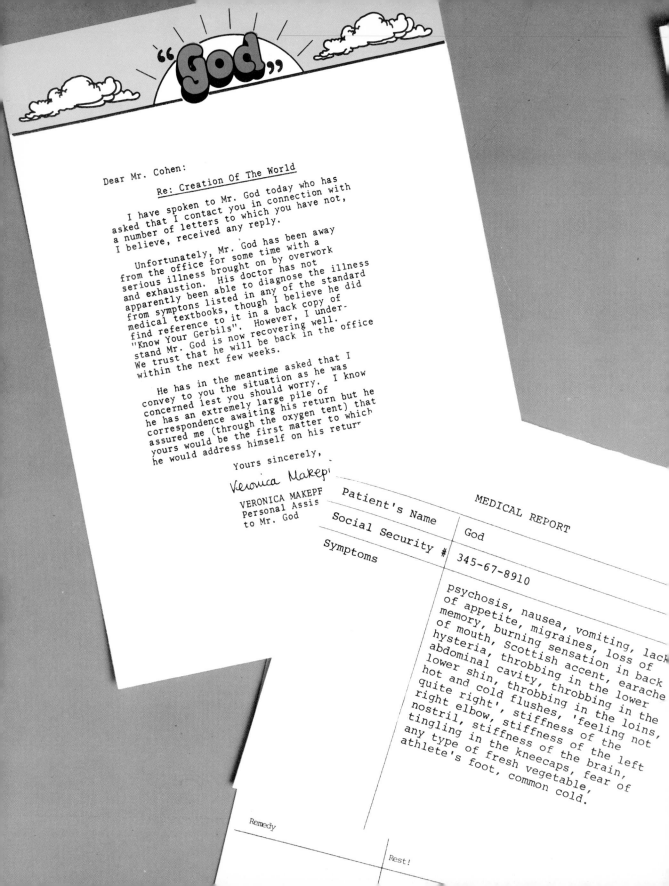

<u>Re: Creation Of The World</u>

I have spoken to Mr. God today who has asked that I contact you in connection with a number of letters to which you have not, I believe, received any reply.

Unfortunately, Mr. God has been away from the office for some time with a serious illness brought on by overwork and exhaustion. His doctor has not apparently been able to diagnose the illness from symptons listed in any of the standard medical textbooks, though I believe he did find reference to it in a back copy of "Know Your Gerbils". However, I understand Mr. God is now recovering well. We trust that he will be back in the office within the next few weeks.

He has in the meantime asked that I convey to you the situation as he was concerned lest you should worry. I know he has an extremely large pile of correspondence awaiting his return but he assured me (through the oxygen tent) that yours would be the first matter to which he would address himself on his retur

Yours sincerely,

Veronica Makep

VERONICA MAKEPF
Personal Assis
to Mr. God

MEDICAL REPORT

Patient's Name	God
Social Security #	345-67-8910
Symptoms	psychosis, nausea, vomiting, lack of appetite, migraines, loss of memory, burning sensation in back of mouth, Scottish accent, earache hysteria, throbbing in the lower abdominal cavity, throbbing in the lower shin, throbbing in the loins, hot and cold flushes, 'feeling not quite right', stiffness of the right elbow, stiffness of the left nostril, stiffness of the brain, tingling in the kneecaps, fear of any type of fresh vegetable, athlete's foot, common cold.
Remedy	Rest!

“God”

Dear Mr. Cohen

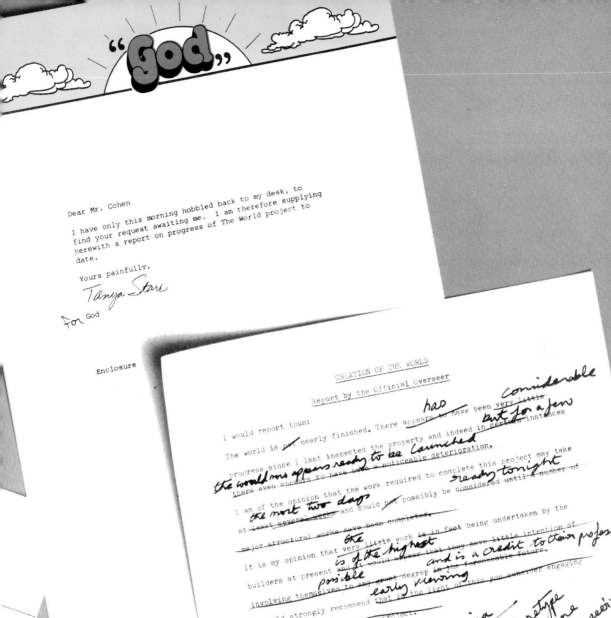

I have only this morning hobbled back to my desk, to find your request awaiting me. I am therefore supplying herewith a report on progress of The World project to date.

Yours painfully,

Tanya Starr

For God

Enclosure

CREATION OF THE WORLD

Report by the Official Overseer

I would report thus:

The world is ~~not~~ nearly finished. There ~~appears to~~ has ~~have~~ been ~~very little~~ considerable progress since I last inspected the property and indeed ~~in certain instances~~ but for a few ~~there even appears to have been a noticeable deterioration.~~ the world now appears ready to be launched

I am of the opinion that the work required to complete this project may take the most two days ~~at least several weeks~~ and could ~~not~~ possibly be considered ready tonight ~~until a number of major structural works have been completed.~~

It is my opinion that ~~very little~~ the work ~~is in fact~~ being undertaken by the builders at present is of the highest possible ~~and it would appear that they have little intention of involving themselves to any great degree in the foreseeable future.~~ and is a credit to their profession

I would strongly recommend ~~that in the light of this you consider engaging new workmen to complete the project.~~ early viewing

Uriah Snooper

Overseer

Veronica

Pse amend and retype as shown. Pass to me for forgery of the overseer's signature, then forward to Cosmic Financial

G

112 GOD G
123498 CONU G

ATTN: GOD

FURTHER TO YOUR REQUEST THAT I VISIT SITE AGAIN, AM PLEASED AND UTTERLY ASTONISHED TO REPORT GOOD = REPEAT GOOD = PROGRESS AT LAST BEING MADE.

THIS IS NOT A HOAX!

WORK WELL ADVANCED. BUILDERS HERE AND WORKING! NO PROBLEMS THAT I CAN SEE, AND I ESTIMATE WELL OVER THREE-QUARTERS OF WORK DONE.

FRANKLY AMAZED.

SUGGEST YOU CONFIRM FOR YOURSELF.

URIAH SNOOPER
OVERSEER

"God"

Dear Mr. Cohen

Re: Creation Of The World

I am sure you will be delighted and relieved to learn that at long last real progress is being made on our project.

My overseer contacted me earlier today with the good news, whereupon I visited the site this afternoon to confirm for myself that the man was not hallucinating. However, the work really is progressing well, and at a good rate.

Needless to say, I am very relieved and am sure you wil feel equally euphoric. I can hardly believe that withi the not-too-distant future we shall at last be ready.

Yours jubilantly,

for, Tanya Starr
God

P.S.
I have, incidentally, attached a number of photographs as proof as I know that you may at this juncture be doubting my sanity.

234987 AMALWORLDS G
112 GOD G
0001/AB

ATTN: T.G. COHEN

WORLD READY BY NOON TOMORROW AT LATEST!

HAVE CONFIRMED WITH THE BUILDERS, WHO INFORM ME THAT JUST ONE DAY'S WORK (ASSEMBLING AND ROAD TESTING MAN AND WOMAN) AT MOST.

TOTALLY OVERWHELMED!

TRUST YOU WILL JOIN ME IN A TOAST.

GOD

112 GOD G
234987 AMALWORLDS G

"God"

Dear Mr. Cohen

Re: Creation Of The World

I fear I may have unfortunately spoken a trifle too soon in my last telex. Having cured all the outstanding technical problems, we were preparing for perhaps the final day's work, at which point a rather petty squabble developed between two groups of workers. It is the kind of thing that happens on building sites all the time, and it is thankfully the sort of thing that usually cools down after a few heated exchanges.

Unfortunately, I'm afraid that in this instance there was little sign of it cooling down, and one of the foremen was therefore asked to step in. In retrospect, his threat of immediate dismissal to all concerned might perhaps be seen as unduly hasty. Certainly that was how the workers saw it, with the unhappy result that we now find ourselves with a strike on our hands. Or rather a strike by our hands.

The dispute originally began, I believe, because those workers concerned with the assembly of Australia felt they were not being paid the same rate as those workers concerned with the assembly of America. Well, to cut a very long story short, it does appear that we are now faced with what will doubtless be a protracted dispute involving management and the two opposing factions. Management won't speak to the workmen. The workmen won't speak to management. The workforce is divided and won't speak to one other. And no one will speak to me.

We have tried all means of reasoning with the workers but without success. I have personally suggested bribery, violence, corruption and garrotting. All to no effect.

We are now therefore at an impasse with all work stopped. I do regret that my earlier jubilation has now had to be curtailed somewhat, but fear the situation was not one I could have anticipated.

With much abject regret,

Tanya Starr

for God

COSMIC FINANCIAL CORPORATION

BIGGEST IN THE UNIVERSE

TELEPHONE:964359214 to 954359792 (inclusive)
TELEX:AMALWORLDS

Dear God:

Re: Creation Of The World

It is with regret that I have to report that Mr. Cohen, with whom I know you have dealt for some considerable time, was today rushed most unexpectedly to the hospital suffering from what the doctors have diagnosed is chronic hysteria.

I believe Mr. Cohen was in the process of reading a letter from you when the attack took place. I know Mr. Cohen wished for me to contact you - indeed, he talked of little else but you on the journey to the hospital. In fact you and blunt instruments seemed to be the only thing he talked about. That was when he spoke. The rest of the journey he spent gazing up at the roof of the ambulance and making strange clucking sounds rather like a hen.

In Mr. Cohen's absence I shall be dealing with all inquiries and I will be in touch with you again as soon as I have had the chance to fully acquaint myself with the situation relating to the World project.

Yours sincerely,

Louis Cheeseberger

LOUIS CHEESEBERGER
Project Development Officer
(Acting)

"God"

Dear Mr. Cheeseberger:

<u>Re: Creation Of The World</u>

Following your request that I put down on paper the points raised during our heated telephone conversation this morning, the situation is as follows:

The deadlock has not been broken yet and, if anything, the position is now even more firmly entrenched.

The workers assembling the vegetation have claimed their work is more arduous than that of those assembling the preformed volcanos and have demanded that their wages be adjusted accordingly.

The workers making the beasts that creepeth have stopped work until they are paid danger money.

The net result is that everyone appears to be in dispute with everybody else. I have attached a list of the workers' additional demands for your reference, and we have appealed to them to return to work pending an inquiry. So far this request has not been met.

Yours moderately,

Veronica Makepiece

for GOD

G:VM

<u>DICTATED BUT NOT READ</u>

"God"

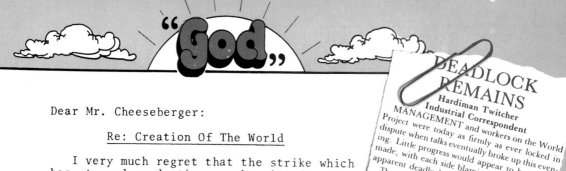

Dear Mr. Cheeseberger:

Re: Creation Of The World

I very much regret that the strike which has stopped production on the site for the last six days is still continuing. In fact, it now shows every sign of becoming rather more ferocious as both sides become all the more militant.

Meanwhile, we have been attracting no little attention from the Press. Needless to say, certain misinformed reporters in the more popular tabloids have taken what I consider to be a biased attitude towards the dispute. I do, however, believe we have fared better with the more informed journals which have at least seen fit to publish our account of things. I fear that this has been an expensive exercise. Freedom of the Press is certainly not cheap these days and I shall shortly be submitting the invoices for my expenses to prove it.

I am enclosing herewith a sample of clippings for your reference.

Yours sincerely,

Veronica Makepeace

for GOD

G:VM

P.S. Glad to hear Mr. Cohen's health is improving, but alarmed to learn he is planning to return to work shortly. Do you think this is wise?

DICTATED BUT NOT READ

DEADLOCK REMAINS

Hardiman Twitcher
Industrial Correspondent

MANAGEMENT and workers on the World Project were today as firmly as ever locked in dispute when talks eventually broke up this evening. Little progress would appear to have been made, with each side blaming the other for the apparent deadlock.

The management are calling for an immediate return to work by all workers while talks continue. The unions are now calling for 43 days of rest a month, a 23-minute working day, and a new bonus scheme. The management has offered the workers an extra half-day... decade and a 17-hour working d... lunch)

SEX SEX SEX

THERE WAS NO SIGN of any sex at all on the picket-line outside The World today as workers continued their industrial action. The dispute, which some have ...

DISPUTE DRAGS ON

AS the dispute at The World project dragged on today, there came news that the workers might decide whether to reconvene earlier talks by the sub-committee ... working party reporting to the permanent com... ...vide special reports.

NO SIGNS OF PEACE

NO SIGNS of peace could be found on the picket-line outside The World today as the workers were described as 'insensitive and uncaring' by their employers.

A spokesman for the workers told me that they were not prepared to st...

PICKETS

Secondary picketing at Th... World today reached epic pro... portions as over 500,000 men joined the striking workers in a show of strength. This "Day of Action", called to sho... pathy of fello... downt...

MANAGEMENT RUSE

A management ruse to employ non-union labour in a bid to complete the work on the ill-fated World Project failed disastrously today when the new non-union workforce employed ...he management decided to-... not to continue work in the ... of mounting threats from ... unions.

... was always a potentially ...rdous scheme and likely to ...e much ill-feeling and ...ntment. A management ...sman branded the strikers ...olent hooligans who had overstepped th...

FASCIST THUGS

THE WORKERS now on 24-hour-a-day picket-duty outside the Creation Project were today branded 'louts, hooligans and complete tits' by Sir Hugo Whippem. Sir Hugo, leader of the 'Kick 'em In The Goolies' Party, called upon the 'stupid, ignorant

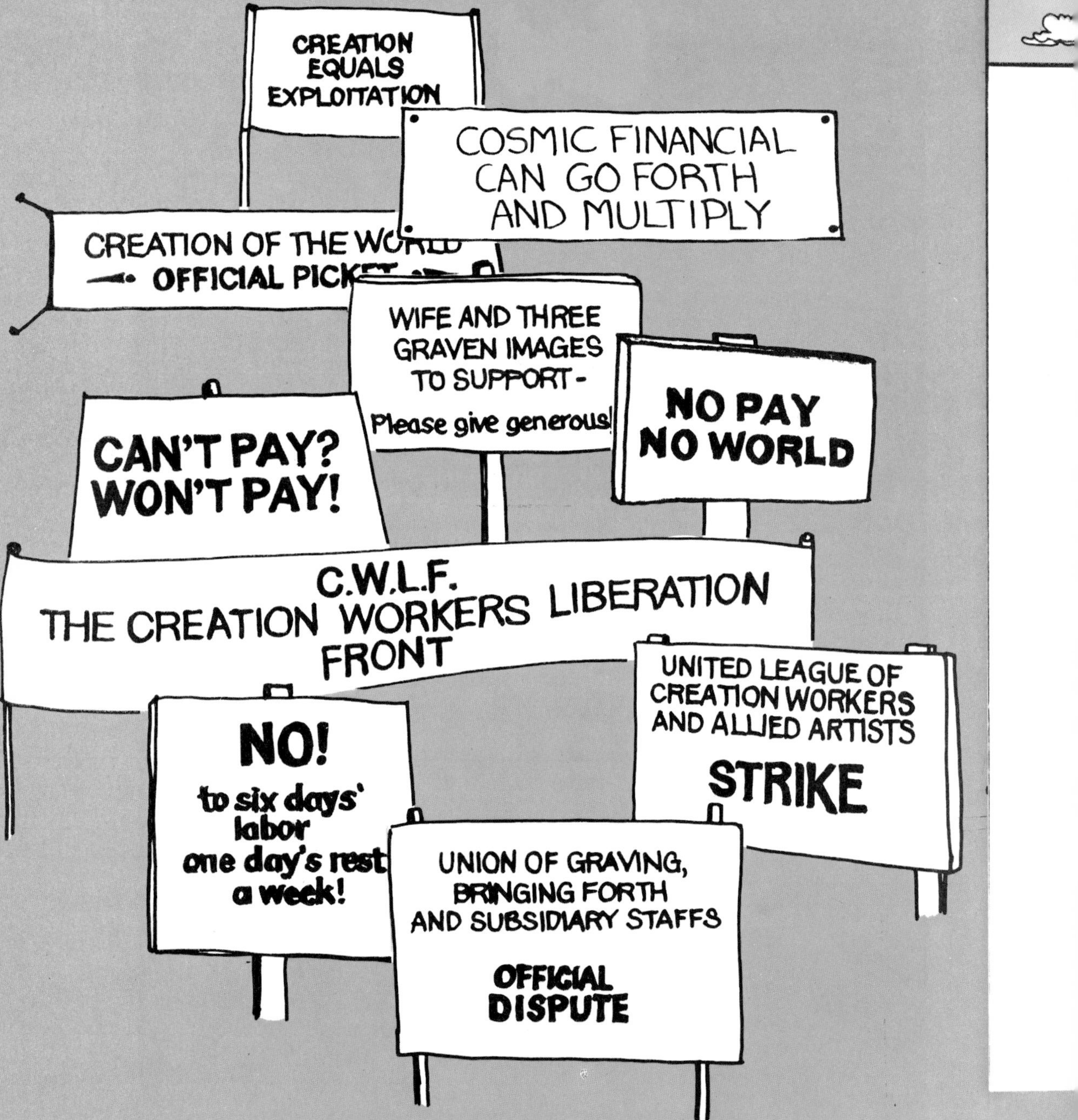

CREATION EQUALS EXPLOITATION
COSMIC FINANCIAL CAN GO FORTH AND MULTIPLY
CREATION OF THE WORLD
OFFICIAL PICK
WIFE AND THREE GRAVEN IMAGES TO SUPPORT -
Please give generous!
NO PAY NO WORLD
CAN'T PAY? WON'T PAY!
C.W.L.F.
THE CREATION WORKERS LIBERATION FRONT
UNITED LEAGUE OF CREATION WORKERS AND ALLIED ARTISTS
STRIKE
NO!
to six days' labor one day's rest a week!
UNION OF GRAVING, BRINGING FORTH AND SUBSIDIARY STAFFS
OFFICIAL DISPUTE

"God"

r. Cohen,

Re: Creation of The World

glad to know you are now fit and
gain. I believe Mr. Cheeseberger
ought you up to date with the
ion on the above, and I'm glad to
e to report what may be cheering

had an illuminating talk yesterday
ur accountants, who informed us of
l loophole they have recently
ered in the law that allows, under
n limited circumstances, for a
to be declared a tax loss which
offset against any tax payable in
n year.

implication is that the strike
onically turn out to be
ially beneficial to the company
ll earn us more than sufficient
to pay any and all of the workers'
s. The accountants are still
g into this area which they do
out is a legal minefield and which
nvolve declaring the world a "Non-
-making Association" for the first
nths of use. It will also involve
aration that all animals and
are bona fide members of one fami

ill report again shortly.

Yours optimistically,

Veronica Makepeace
for GOD

ED BUT NOT READ

"God"

Dear Mr. Cohen:

As we had hoped, the accountants have been able to make use of the considerable legal loophole referred to in my previous letter and we are now thankfully approaching an end to the dispute.

Unfortunately, due to some legal formality about which I am not too clear, we now have to ensure the strike lasts for a minimum of forty-one consecutive days. Since we are now on the thirty-sixth day it was ironical that the workmen should have chosen this of all days to throw in the towel and return to work. Needless to say, we have resisted this move in order to retain the large financial benefit to be gained from a lengthy tax-deductible strike. We have therefore stated that under no circumstances can we take the workers back, and have set out new stringent terms which I feel sure they will turn down. In this way, we hope to be able to avoid any settlement for at least the next five days.

Yours deviously,

Veronica Makepeace
for GOD

G:VM

DICTATED BUT NOT READ

Dear Mr. Cohen:

Two days to go to the end of the dispute, and misfortune has struck again. Just when we looked set for the tax dodge to come our way, the workers have let us down by accepting our new terms! They are at this moment preparing to return to work and my only chance is to insist on further clauses. But it will be difficult. Already we have reduced the workers' wages to virtually nil with just one day's rest a month. I will use my best endeavors but must warn you that, unless we are very lucky, it does look as though the strike may be all over within the hour.

Yours pessimistically,

Veronica Makepiece

Dear Mr. Cohen:

We've done it! The workforce was practically suicidal in its desire to return to work and I dare say we could not have held out a day longer. But it matters not, because our forty-one days are up and we have just this moment negotiated for the workers to return to their tasks by lunchtime (while we pocket a very tidy sum, courtesy of the tax codes, in the process).

I cannot tell you what a relief it is to have the whole incident safely behind us for, although we have achieved rich pickings in the face of adversity, it was not an episode I would care to repeat. In addition, we are now a further 41 days behind schedule.

Nevertheless, we are now "back on the rails," so to speak. And far richer in the process.

Yours affluently,

Veronica Makepiece

"God"

Dear Mr. Cohen:

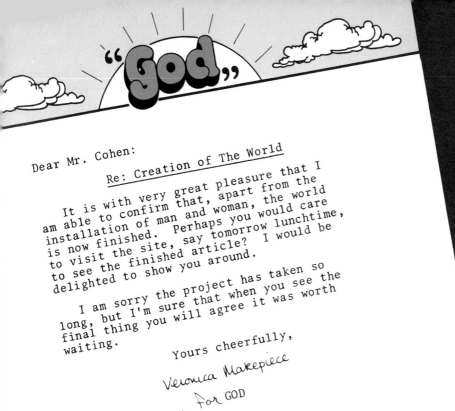

Re: Creation of The World

It is with very great pleasure that I am able to confirm that, apart from the installation of man and woman, the world is now finished. Perhaps you would care to visit the site, say tomorrow lunchtime, to see the finished article? I would be delighted to show you around.

I am sorry the project has taken so long, but I'm sure that when you see the final thing you will agree it was worth waiting.

Yours cheerfully,

Veronica Makepiece

for GOD

G:VM

DICTATED BUT

112 GOD G
123498 CONU G

ATTN: GOD

PLEASED TO REPORT WORLD V.V.V NEARLY COMPLETE. APART FROM ASSEMBLY AND INSTALLATION OF MAN AND WOMAN HAVE PRACTICALLY FINISHED. ESTIMATE WE WILL FINISH TOMORROW LUNCHTIME AT LATEST.

CAN WE HAVE MONEY?

REGARDS

TED SLAGWORTHY

123498 CONU G
112 GOD G

112 GOD G

234987 AMALWORLDS G

0001/AB

ATTN: GOD

YOUR LATEST LETTER INDICATES IMMINENT COMPLETION OF WORLD PROJECT.

FRANKLY HIGHLY SKEPTICAL!

HAVE HEARD IT ALL BEFORE.

SOUNDS TO ME LIKE ANOTHER PIECE OF WISHFUL THINKING.

NOT AT ALL SURE I BELIEVE A WORD YOU SAY.

WITHHOLDING ANY COMMENT AT THIS STAGE!

T.G. COHEN

234987 AMALWORLDS G

112 GOD G

UNIVERSAL CONSTRUCTION CO.

General Builders & Contractors

3rd Arch Along
Limepit Viaduct
Telephone 18194804612 (one line)
Telex CONU

MEMBER OF THE FEDERATION OF SMALL BUILDERS AND BUILDING CONTRACTORS

Dear God:

Re: Creation of The World

You will recall from our last conversation that we had only a relatively minor matter to attend to, namely the manufacture, assembly and installation of man and woman. I regret to report that we have suffered a number of problems with this work.

Our first trouble was caused when the manufacturers informed us that they had lost the drawings you had supplied. Not wishing to upset you or cause you unnecessary trouble, we sent them a few sketches that we executed ourselves. We also provided a few additional details. However, I'm afraid the results were not perhaps quite what we had anticipated. Apart from a rather upsetting grin and a complete lack of hair, the man and woman turned out to be mechanically unsound and totally impossible to control. We found the leg mechanism rather difficult to assemble, with the result that the man and woman kept falling over. In the end I'm afraid we were forced to affix casters to their feet, which certainly cured the problem but did lead to a slightly ungainly way of walking. Neither the man nor the woman's head would balance on their shoulders and kept rolling off. In addition, we discovered the ears were coming away from their fixing bolts.

Finally, we have discovered that the wings which we had hoped to incorporate are somewhat impractical and we have therefore decided to disregard the "flight" specification. We are sure you will approve of this slight modification particularly since it will allow us to complete the work more rapidly.

Yours unfortunately,

Gwyn MacTaggart (Secretary)

TED SLAGWORTHY
For Universal Construction Co.

112 GOD G
123498 CONU G

ATTN: GOD

HAVE DISCOVERED MAN'S BRAIN FITTED WRONG WAY ROUND. HE'S NOW WALKING AND TALKING BACKWARDS. REPLACEMENT BRAIN ON ORDER.

HIS EYES NOT WORKING CORRECTLY EITHER AND AS A RESULT HAS HAD A NUMBER OF RATHER SERIOUS ACCIDENTS WHICH HAVE PUT US BACK SLIGHTLY.

ALSO SERIOUS IMBALANCE IN DIGESTIVE SYSTEM. HEAVY-DUTY FACE MASKS AND RESPIRATORS ON ORDER ... MUST DASH, CAN HEAR HIM COMING.

TED SLAGWORTHY

123498 CONU G
112 GOD G

123498 CONU G

ATTN: GOD

NOW FITTED MAN'S REPLACEMENT BRAIN. DIGESTIVE SYSTEM NOW FUNCTIONING PROPERLY, THANK GOODNESS. EYES IMPROVING.

NEW PROPLEM, HOWEVER...WOMAN UNABLE TO STOP WHISTLING. QUITE PLEASANT FOR FIRST FIVE MINUTES, BUT NOW UNBEARABLE. HAVE TRIED BAND-AIDS, BUT TO NO EFFECT. HAVE ALSO TRIED LARGE HAMMER, WHICH HAD SLIGHTLY MORE EFFECT.

IS REGAINING CONSCIOUSNESS NOW, AND AM CONSIDERING REMOVAL OF HER TEETH. IT'S OUR LAST HOPE.

112 GOD G
123498 CONU G

ATTN: GOD

HAVE CURED ALL PROBLEMS. WOMAN STOPPED WHISTLING. BOTH MAN AND WOMAN NOW WALKING/TALKING/EATING AS REQUIRED.

AM PREPARING TO TAKE BOTH ON ROAD TEST.

WILL REPORT.

TED SLAGWORTH

123498 CONU G
112 GOD G

112 GOD G
123498 CONU G

ATTN: GOD

ROAD TEST ON MAN NOT TOO SUCCESSFUL. HE'S UNABLE TO NEGOTIATE SHARP CORNERS. CANNOT GO UPHILL. AFRAID TO GO INTO REVERSE.

ALSO TENDS TO LIMP BADLY, ESPECIALLY AFTER WALKING INTO FIRE HYDRANTS. (ALSO COMPLAINS A LOT, ESPECIALLY AFTER WALKING INTO FIRE HYDRANTS. AND NOW SINGS SOPRANO).

ADJUSTMENTS BEING MADE.

TED SLAGWORTHY

123498 CONU G
112 GOD G

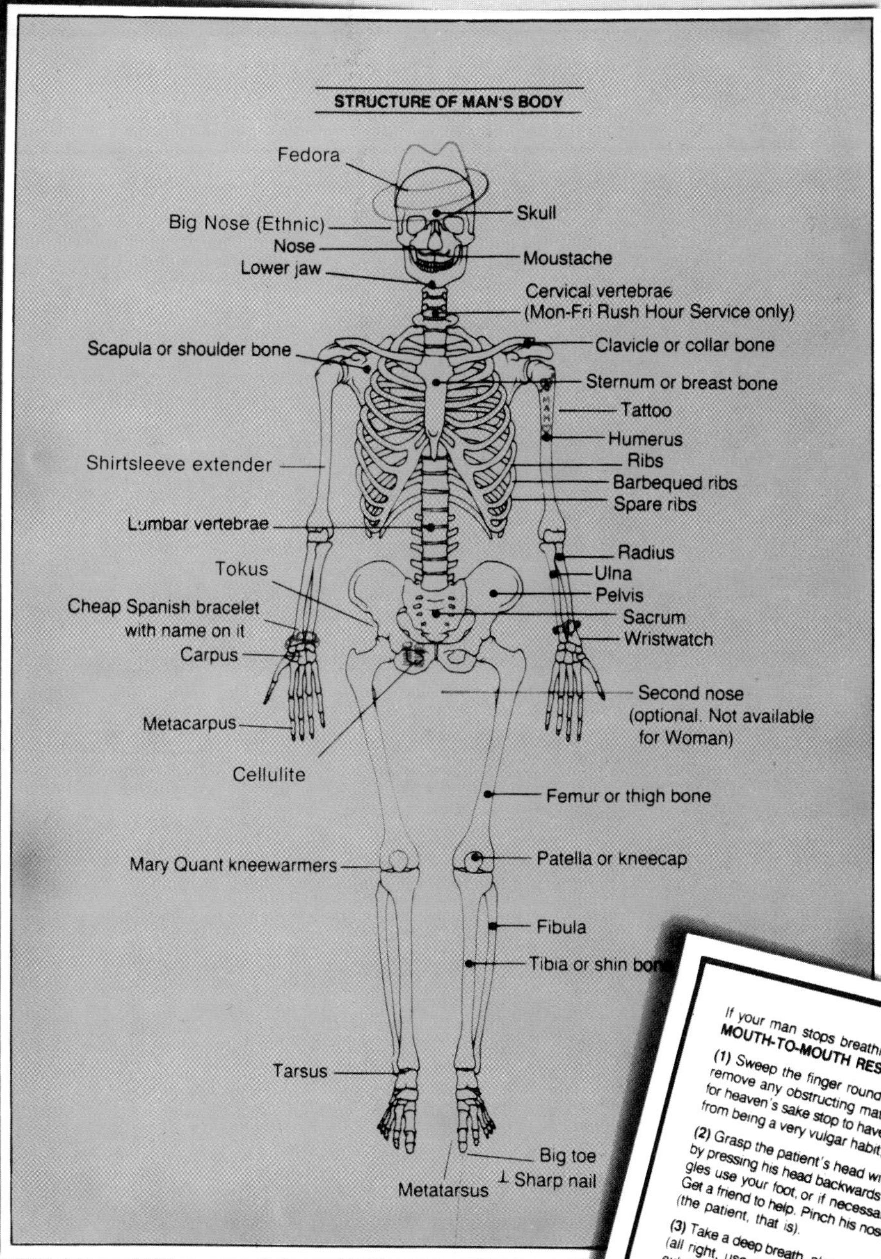

If your man stops breathing...

MOUTH-TO-MOUTH RESUSCITATION

(1) Sweep the finger round the back of the patient's mouth to remove any obstructing matter. Don't take too long. And don't for heaven's sake stop to have a look at what you've found. Apart from being a very vulgar habit, you are also losing vital seconds.

(2) Grasp the patient's head with one hand and extend his neck by pressing his head backwards with your other hand. If he struggles use your foot, or if necessary both feet, to keep him down. Get a friend to help. Pinch his nose shut and hold his mouth open (the patient, that is).

(3) Take a deep breath, place your mouth over the patient's mouth (all right, use a handkerchief if it makes you feel happier) and exhale forcibly into his lungs. Try not to cough or burp at this point. Chest expansion should be observed.

(4) Withdraw the mouth and take another deep breath while the man exhales. Don't laugh or make jokes about what's going on – the patient may be listening. Repeat the cycle 10 to 12 times a minute. The first six breaths should be given as rapidly as possible. But don't be silly and try to rush it – it's not a game.

(5) When the man comes round, tell him what you've done. He may like to give you some money for helping him.

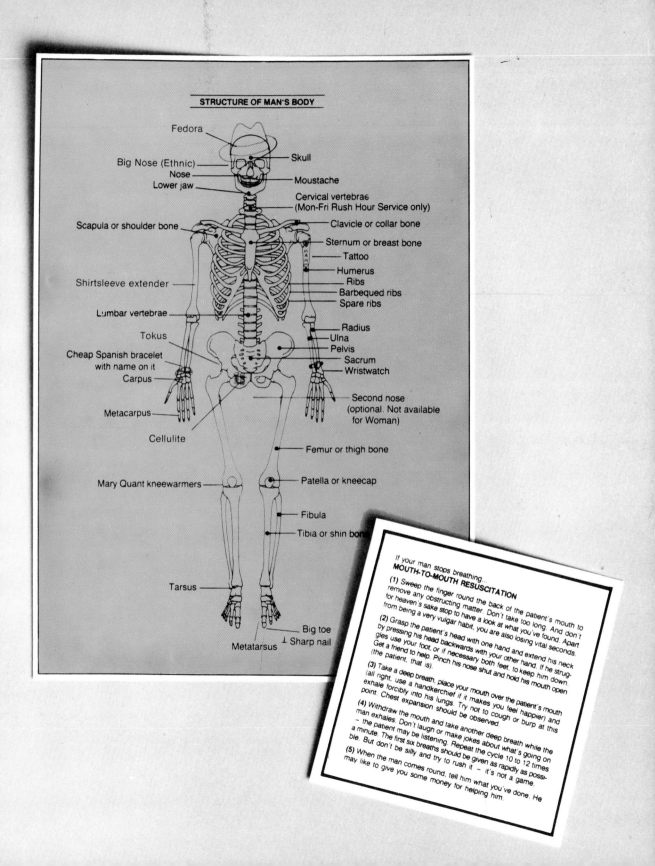

“God”

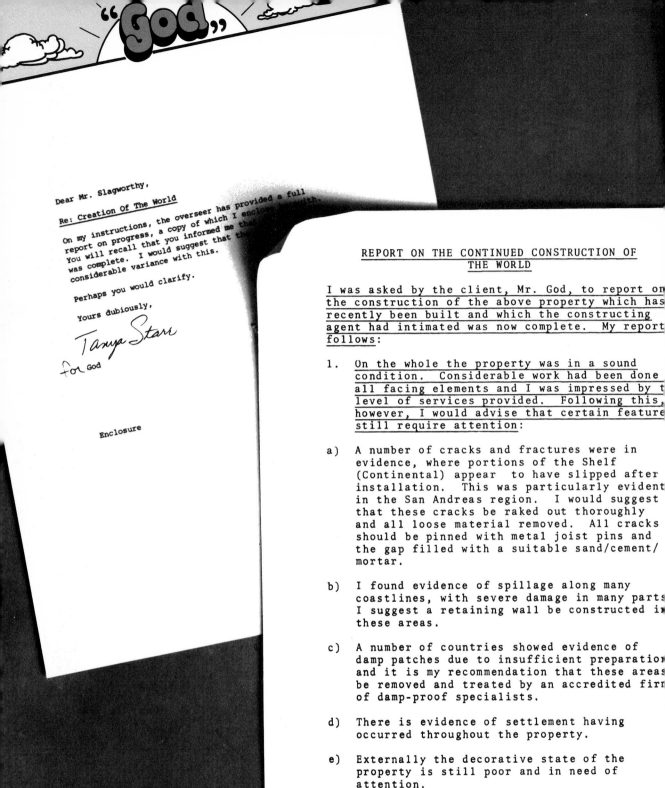

Dear Mr. Slagworthy,

Re: Creation Of The World

On my instructions, the overseer has provided a full report on progress, a copy of which I enclo[illegible]with. You will recall that you informed me th[illegible] was complete. I would suggest that th[illegible] considerable variance with this.

Perhaps you would clarify.

Yours dubiously,

Tanya Starr

for God

Enclosure

REPORT ON THE CONTINUED CONSTRUCTION OF THE WORLD

I was asked by the client, Mr. God, to report on the construction of the above property which has recently been built and which the constructing agent had intimated was now complete. My report follows:

1. On the whole the property was in a sound condition. Considerable work had been done all facing elements and I was impressed by t level of services provided. Following this, however, I would advise that certain feature still require attention:

a) A number of cracks and fractures were in evidence, where portions of the Shelf (Continental) appear to have slipped after installation. This was particularly evident in the San Andreas region. I would suggest that these cracks be raked out thoroughly and all loose material removed. All cracks should be pinned with metal joist pins and the gap filled with a suitable sand/cement/ mortar.

b) I found evidence of spillage along many coastlines, with severe damage in many parts I suggest a retaining wall be constructed in these areas.

c) A number of countries showed evidence of damp patches due to insufficient preparation and it is my recommendation that these areas be removed and treated by an accredited firm of damp-proof specialists.

d) There is evidence of settlement having occurred throughout the property.

e) Externally the decorative state of the property is still poor and in need of attention.

f) No comment as to the function of the sanitaryware can be made, as the water was turned off at the time of my inspection.

112 GOD G
123498 CONU G

ATTN: GOD

DELIGHTED TO REPORT THAT WORLD IS AT LONG LAS
COMPLETE = REPEAT WORLD COMPLETE!

KINDEST REGARDS.

TED SLAGWORTHY

123498 CONU G
112 GOD G

ATTN: TED SLAGWORTHY

HAVE YOU BEEN HITTING THE BOTTLE? AM I DREAMING?
CAN IT BE TRUE?

PLEASE CONFIRM YOUR LATEST TELEX WAS NOT A CRUEL
JOKE. IS WORLD REALLY COMPLETE?

GOD

112 GOD G
123498 CONU G

ATTN: GOD

PREVIOUS TELEX QUITE CORRECT. YOUR SKEPTICISM
UNDERSTANDABLE. CAN HARDLY BELIEVE IT MYSELF.

TED

112 GOD G
123498 CONU G

112 GOD G
123498 CONU G

ATTN: GOD

FURTHER TO YOUR REQUEST THAT I VISIT SITE TO
CONFIRM EARLIER REPORTS AND TO MAKE SURE THAT THEY
WEREN'T LYING, AM AT SITE AND IT'S ALL TRUE!
WORK REALLY IS FINISHED.

WILD PARTY NOW IN PROGRESS ... MUST GO.

VERONICA MAKEPEACE

GOD G
0001/AB

ATTN: T.G. COHEN

ECSTATIC TO REPORT THAT WORLD IS FINALLY COMPLETE, DOWN
TO THE VERY LAST DETAIL. HAVE CHECKED, RECHECKED AND
DOUBLE-CHECKED THAT THIS IS SO.

CHAMPAGNE TO FOLLOW.

KINDEST REGARDS.

GOD

"God"

Dear Mr. Cohen:

Re: Creation of The World

You were, I am sure, most relieved to learn that The World is now complete.

Looking back, of course, one must confess that a period of six working days in which to complete all the work was perhaps a trifle ambitious, and in the future when we come to create new worlds together, as I'm sure we shall, I suggest we perhaps be a little more realistic with our schedules. I think, too, that we might perhaps have allowed our enthusiasm to run away with us on one or two other aspects, notably the man and woman.

However, I'm sure that we won't let the few upsetting incidents along the way mar the many, many hours of happiness which the project has given us.

I trust that you and your wife will call in at my office when you are next in town. I would be delighted to see you both and to take you out to lunch.

With my most sincere regards,

G

GOD

UNIVERSAL CONSTRUCTION CO.
General Builders & Contractors

3rd Arch Along
Limepit Viaduct
Telephone 18194804612 (one line)
Telex CONU

MEMBER OF THE FEDERATION OF SMALL BUILDERS
AND BUILDING CONTRACTORS

...ar God:

...: Creation of The World

...ease find enclosed our invoice for the ...rk completed on the above project. As you ...ill see, we have itemized the various costs ...nvolved. The final amount is slightly more ...han we had originally estimated but I am ...ure you will agree the costs are realistic, ...earing in mind the amount of work involved.

I trust you will find the costs to your satisfaction and will arrange for a speedy settlement.

Would it be possible for a check to be sent by return mail?

With kindest regards,

Gwyn MacTaggart (Secretary)

TED SLAGWORTHY
Universal Construction Co.
(BUILDERS OF BRAND NEW WORLD)

Dear Mr. Slagworthy:

Re: Creation Of The World

I have received your letter and invoice. There is not the slightest prospect of you receiving settlement in the foreseeable or unforeseeable future.

May I remind you that the work you carried out was late, poor and in breach of all contracts you signed.

I have no intention of even considering your invoice until I return from vacation in six years, by which time you can be assured that I will have forgotten it completely.

I trust you will find this to your satisfaction.

Yours sarcastically,

7 5 6 4
2 5 1 6 3 7 2 2 8
5 7 4 6 2 8 2 0 1 8 5 7 6
6 7 4 0 3 9 5 8 2 2 4 1 6 3 7 2 6
4 8 5 7 1 0 2 9 4 8 5 7 6 8 4 8 4 8 3 6 4
4 7 5 8 6 9 2 0 3 9 0 4 9 5 7 2 8 1 2 4 3 5 5 4 7 6
9 4 8 5 7 2 9 6 8 4 7 5 6 3 9 5 8 3 7 5 6 2 0 0 0 0 9

476,831,298,354,587,683,509,352,546,657,233,441,552

(Gratuity not included)

SHUSTER, SHYSTER, SUSHI, and POLLOCK

Attorneys at Law

Dear Mr. Slagworthy,

Re: Creation Of The World

As you no doubt remember, we act as attorney for Mr. God and have been asked by him to supply you with the enclosed 980-page legal resume. I would be grateful if you would read and return this to us, together with any points you may wish to make. This is essential to opening of negotiations regarding settlement arising from works undertaken.

Failure to reply satisfactorily within two days will be deemed as forfeiture of all your rights to settlement.

Yours lawfully.

P.P. Scribbling

P.P. Scribbling (Partner)

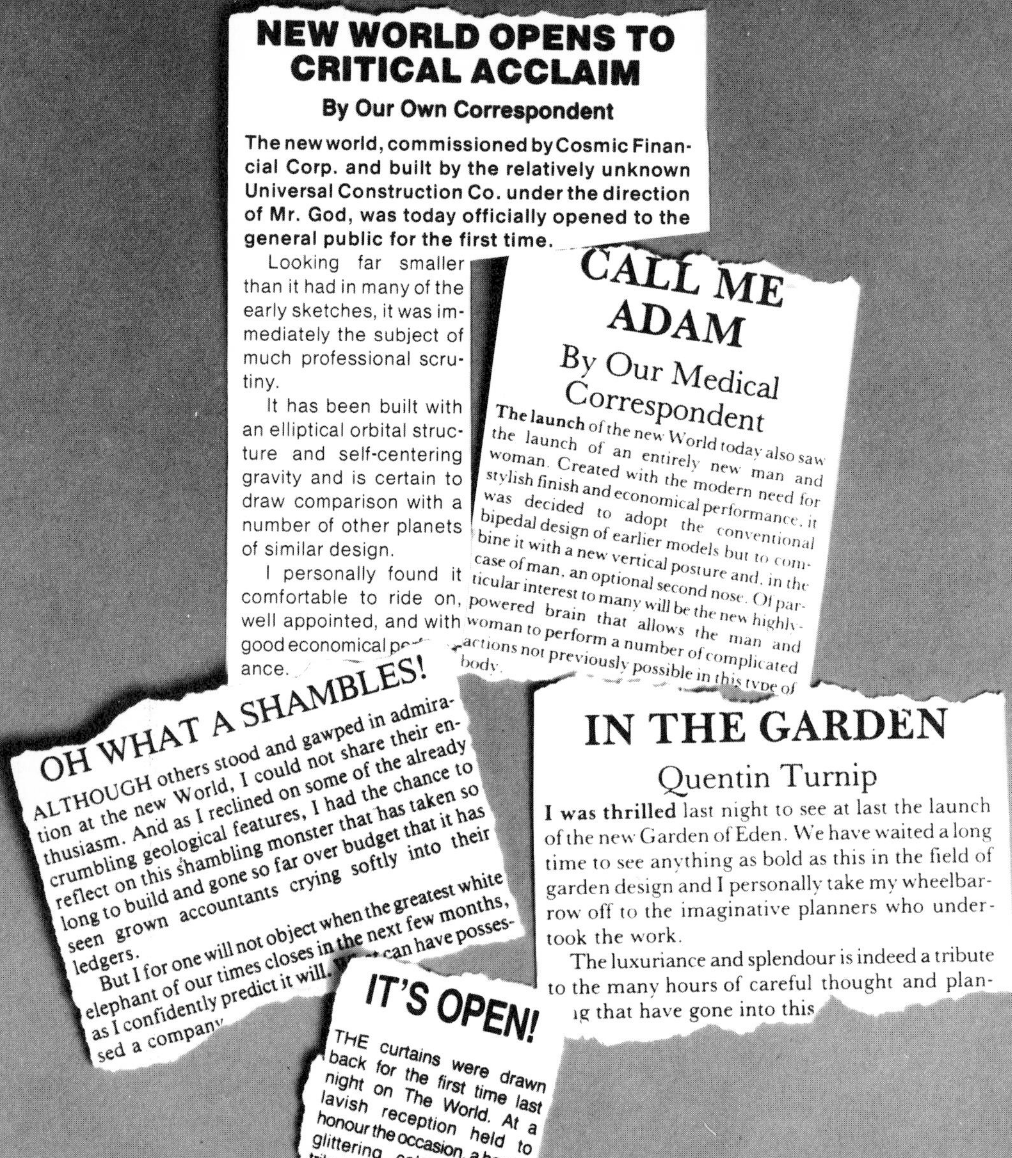

NEW WORLD OPENS TO CRITICAL ACCLAIM

By Our Own Correspondent

The new world, commissioned by Cosmic Financial Corp. and built by the relatively unknown Universal Construction Co. under the direction of Mr. God, was today officially opened to the general public for the first time.

Looking far smaller than it had in many of the early sketches, it was immediately the subject of much professional scrutiny.

It has been built with an elliptical orbital structure and self-centering gravity and is certain to draw comparison with a number of other planets of similar design.

I personally found it comfortable to ride on, well appointed, and with good economical per... ance.

CALL ME ADAM

By Our Medical Correspondent

The launch of the new World today also saw the launch of an entirely new man and woman. Created with the modern need for stylish finish and economical performance, it was decided to adopt the conventional bipedal design of earlier models but to combine it with a new vertical posture and, in the case of man, an optional second nose. Of particular interest to many will be the new highly-powered brain that allows the man and woman to perform a number of complicated actions not previously possible in this type of body.

OH WHAT A SHAMBLES!

ALTHOUGH others stood and gawped in admiration at the new World, I could not share their enthusiasm. And as I reclined on some of the already crumbling geological features, I had the chance to reflect on this shambling monster that has taken so long to build and gone so far over budget that it has seen grown accountants crying softly into their ledgers.

But I for one will not object when the greatest white elephant of our times closes in the next few months, as I confidently predict it will. W... can have possessed a company...

IN THE GARDEN

Quentin Turnip

I was thrilled last night to see at last the launch of the new Garden of Eden. We have waited a long time to see anything as bold as this in the field of garden design and I personally take my wheelbarrow off to the imaginative planners who undertook the work.

The luxuriance and splendour is indeed a tribute to the many hours of careful thought and plan...ng that have gone into this

IT'S OPEN!

THE curtains were drawn back for the first time last night on The World. At a lavish reception held to honour the occasion, a host of glittering celebrities paid tribute to the great endeavou... that has bee...

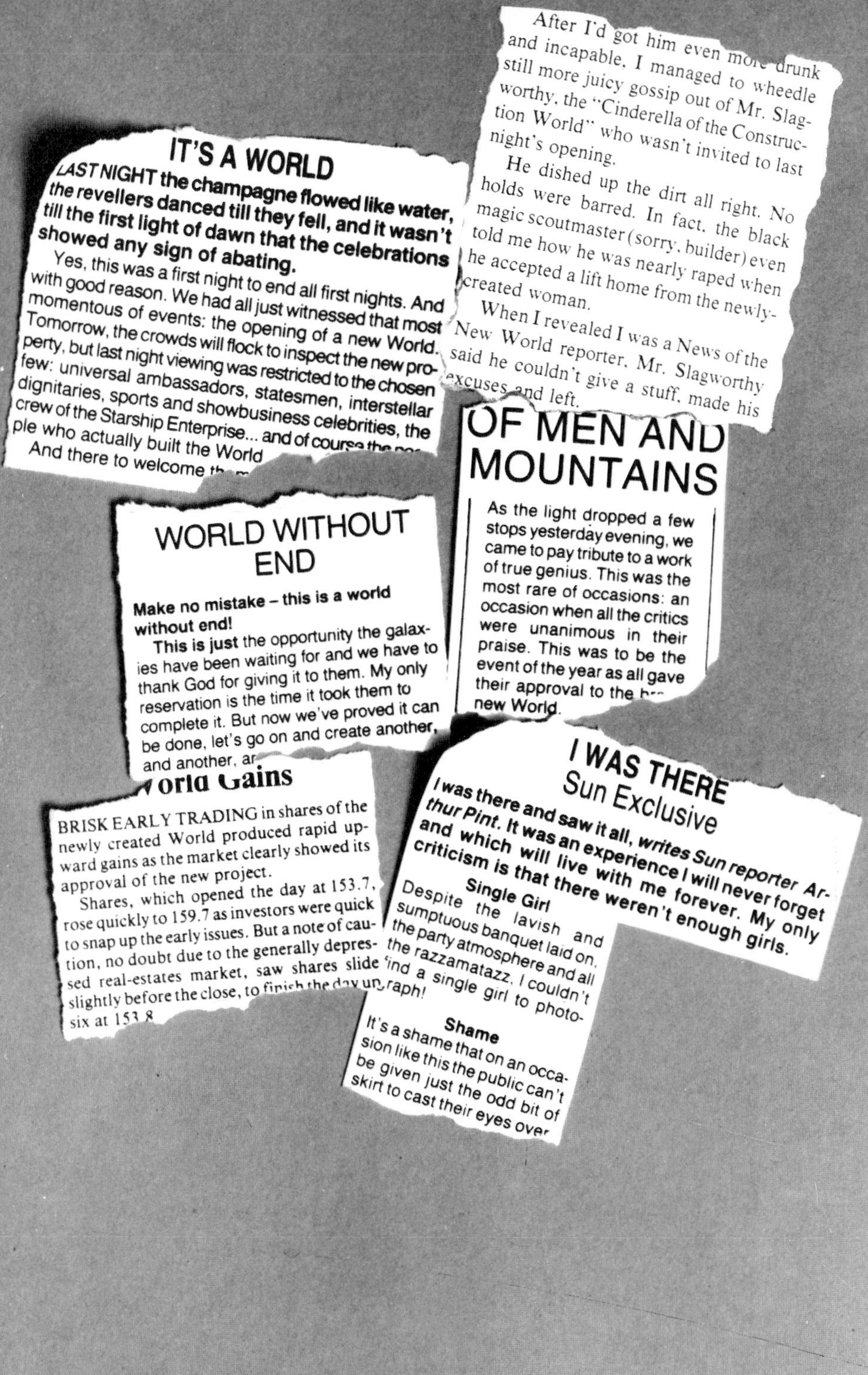

IT'S A WORLD

LAST NIGHT the champagne flowed like water, the revellers danced till they fell, and it wasn't till the first light of dawn that the celebrations showed any sign of abating.

Yes, this was a first night to end all first nights. And with good reason. We had all just witnessed that most momentous of events: the opening of a new World. Tomorrow, the crowds will flock to inspect the new property, but last night viewing was restricted to the chosen few: universal ambassadors, statesmen, interstellar dignitaries, sports and showbusiness celebrities, the crew of the Starship Enterprise... and of course the peo-ple who actually built the World

And there to welcome th...

After I'd got him even more drunk and incapable, I managed to wheedle still more juicy gossip out of Mr. Slagworthy, the "Cinderella of the Construction World" who wasn't invited to last night's opening.

He dished up the dirt all right. No holds were barred. In fact, the black magic scoutmaster (sorry, builder) even told me how he was nearly raped when he accepted a lift home from the newly-created woman.

When I revealed I was a News of the New World reporter, Mr. Slagworthy said he couldn't give a stuff, made his excuses and left.

OF MEN AND MOUNTAINS

As the light dropped a few stops yesterday evening, we came to pay tribute to a work of true genius. This was the most rare of occasions: an occasion when all the critics were unanimous in their praise. This was to be the event of the year as all gave their approval to the br... new World.

WORLD WITHOUT END

Make no mistake – this is a world without end!

This is just the opportunity the galaxies have been waiting for and we have to thank God for giving it to them. My only reservation is the time it took them to complete it. But now we've proved it can be done, let's go on and create another, and another, ar...

...orld Gains

BRISK EARLY TRADING in shares of the newly created World produced rapid upward gains as the market clearly showed its approval of the new project.

Shares, which opened the day at 153.7, rose quickly to 159.7 as investors were quick to snap up the early issues. But a note of caution, no doubt due to the generally depressed real-estates market, saw shares slide slightly before the close, to finish the day up six at 153.8

I WAS THERE
Sun Exclusive

***I was there and saw it all, writes Sun reporter Arthur Pint.* It was an experience I will never forget and which will live with me forever. My only criticism is that there weren't enough girls.**

Single Girl

Despite the lavish and sumptuous banquet laid on, the party atmosphere and all the razzamatazz, I couldn't find a single girl to photograph!

Shame

It's a shame that on an occasion like this the public can't be given just the odd bit of skirt to cast their eyes over

Dear God,

I am writing to ask whether something can't be done to stop the large number of people using our road as a short cut on the way to your world. This used to be a quiet street where the

Dear God,

I thought you might like to know that your new world appears to be leaking a rather nasty brown liquid. In addition, my wife tells me

Dear God,

I am writing to you in connection with your new world which, I was alarmed to notice, appears to be emitting dense clouds of black, pungent smoke. I hope that this is

Dear God,

Recently I have noticed a strange smell which I can only identify as coming from your new world, and I trust that you will visit the site as I am concerned that it may be toxic and could be polluting the

Dear Sir:

This morning I was outraged to find a large mountain in my garden. It would appear to have fallen off your world, and I insist that you call round to remove the offending object immediately.

Dear Sir:

My family was upset this morning to see a strang
man walking around our neighborhood. He had a "he
and, strange though it may seem, appeared to be
walking on two legs, so I can only assume he was
from your new world. I'd be grateful if you cou
insure that this sort of incident does not occu
again, as it only frightens the children and u
the wife.